AN INTRODUCTION TO

CHAKROLOGY™ –

CHAKRA THEORY, THERAPY AND BALANCING

JEREMY JONES

PUBLISHED BY THE YOGA COLLEGE, WITHAM, ESSEX UK

AN INTRODUCTION TO CHAKROLOGY™ – CHAKRA THEORY, THERAPY AND BALANCING.

© Jeremy Jones August 2010

All Rights Reserved

ISBN 978-0-9551076-3-4

First published September 2010 by
The Yoga College,
10 Hazel Close,
Witham, Essex, UK.

AN INTRODUCTION TO CHAKROLOGY™ – CHAKRA THEORY, THERAPY AND BALANCING

I dedicate this book to all those who research the life energy, by whatever name. It is a lonely furrow you plough - but plough it you must...

"Man has no body distinct from his soul..."

William Blake.

CONTENTS

ACKNOWLEDGEMENTS

Every writer and researcher stands on somebody else's shoulders. I am no exception. What is often overlooked is that, as he stands rather unsteadily on those shoulders, there are many hands holding him safely with words of encouragement and inspiration, snippets of information and sometimes, a considerable amount of finite time and energy, freely sacrificed. To all these people, who I list in no particular order (apart from the first), I must offer my heartfelt thanks - and my apologies for any inadvertent omissions.

- Diane Bitmead, my partner, for her love, support, encouragement and computer advice. Also for her considerable time spent on proof reading and providing an occasional informal kinesiology "slant" to the subject matter and her time spent as my principal "guinea pig". More importantly, for putting up with my constant state of distraction as I obsess over my creative pregnancy.

- My students who have also volunteered as guinea pigs and offered useful "info titbits", especially my student teachers (now with a well deserved qualification) – Janice Dawkins, Leigh-Acteson-Rook, Claire Reynolds, Sarah Pettitt, Joani St. Cliere, Caroline Hall, Christine Hare and Josie Jupp.

- My brother Peter Jones, who taught me most of what I know about the work of Wilhelm Reich and encouraged my research, which I must confess is a little feeble, compared to his titanic efforts but I was able to illustrate and reinforce my points on life energy, build an orac (more on that later) and practice self-treatment – a double bonus.

- San Story and Richard Warner, who have both given me useful ideas and thoughts on the "Sino-Indian connection", the cultural and functional overlap between Indian Yoga and Chinese qigong and tai chi.

- David Marett of *Heliognosis*, who made my life energy meter and supplied useful software, advice and data retrieval hardware.

- My teaching diploma tutor, Ian Burgess who first demonstrated the pendulum technique to me.

INTRODUCTION

This book makes no pretence at being "learned" or "academic", even though it is the result of a considerable amount of thought and investigation. It is a straightforward guide to a subject that many find intriguing yet baffling. It is aimed mainly at the complementary therapist who would like an "extra string to the bow", the yoga teacher or student and anyone else with an interest in the psycho-physical. I hesitate to use the term "spiritual", even though it is an entirely valid one because, all too often, it is used in a meaningless, befogging way – so we are left with a rather ugly "psycho-jargon" expression. It will have to do. Chakras are often correctly described as "psycho-physical centres". They are influenced by the mind and emotions and conversely, the mind and emotions are influenced by the chakras in an elegant and logical two-way flow. As we shall see, another valid definition would be "psycho-energetic centres" or "life energy vortices". The literal meaning of the Sanskrit word is "wheel", so "life energy flywheel" might be another possible label.

A few words about my own approach might be in order. Despite my background, this is not really a book about yoga. It is about one aspect of the yoga tradition that has jumped out of the box and into general "alternative" or "new age" thinking and therapy. I have few literary *bêtes noires* - good writing is good writing - but one of them is an excess of technical terminology and abbreviations, which in my opinion is unconsciously designed with a hidden, elitist agenda, namely to prevent curious outsiders and enthusiastic beginners from learning too much. When I worked at a college, which shall remain nameless, I was in receipt of a weekly newsletter that was incomprehensible, due to it being peppered with jargon, abbreviations and acronyms. It was regularly binned by me, accompanied by various unprintable expletives! For an education establishment to produce such a document is frankly disgraceful and accentuated my distaste for such opaque writing. I do not use or speak that strange dialect of the English language I call Academicese. However, we must "get real". Occasional technical terms are essential for clarity but I have tried always to give a "plain English" alternative in brackets. There is also an explanatory glossary of terms that may be unfamiliar to the reader. I have not made any assumptions about prior knowledge, so I trust those who are blessed with such knowledge will forgive occasional statements of the obvious. Keep reading - there's plenty in the book you won't know! To paraphrase a joke I used on the cover of *"A Yoga Garland"*, this book contains "everything you didn't know you didn't know" about chakras. When I used that term, I was unaware of its use by a certain politician who later became notorious for his ineptitude. Ah well, you can't keep a bad idea down!

There are a few things that have been deliberately omitted or heavily abbreviated. This is usually because the material sources are so confused and mystified that any contribution by me will simply add to the confusion or because the subject, e.g. associated deities, is purely a matter of personal belief, rather than something of therapeutic value.

A final, important point. This is not a science book but it contains many references to science, though that science is sometimes little known or appreciated. I have tried to approach the subject as much as possible from an evidence base, even though that evidence would not always satisfy the demands of hard science. There is still much work to be done on researching the chakras and life energy in general but that, as they say, is another story.

Whatever your path in life, work and knowledge, I wish you well.

1. BACKGROUND

I first came across the chakras when I was studying to be a yoga teacher in 1993. The idea of life energy has been familiar to me for much longer, since the 1960s, but more about that later. My reaction to both concepts was the same – "fascinating, but what use is it?" I've always had a strongly practical streak in my makeup and, when younger, little patience with philosophy, mysticism or abstract theorising. During my teacher-training course, the tutor demonstrated the location of the chakras, using an improvised pendulum. I was intrigued but put it to the back of my mind as being of little practical use, as opposed to other yoga practices, which most definitely *do* have a practical use in the field of personal development and well-being. At this stage, I must ask readers who are not interested in yoga to bear with me. It is impossible to avoid the fact that the birthplace of chakra theory lies firmly within the yoga tradition, even though it is used now in many other disciplines. Further, my "route of discovery" was charted through yoga. I have been unable to find reliable evidence of similar theories in other traditional non-western disciplines but I would not be surprised if such evidence does exist. Yoga is most certainly not the only repository of wisdom and it does not exist in a vacuum, despite assertions to the contrary by a few of its more fundamentalist enthusiasts.

Some years after my training, I was asked by the organisation concerned to tutor a foundation course for yoga enthusiasts who wanted to "dig deeper". In my opinion, the syllabus had one glaring fault. I was asked to teach my students bija mantra (chants or sounds to stimulate and open the chakras) without teaching them anything at all about the chakras themselves. This was rather like trying to train an aspiring concert pianist advanced techniques before they could read music. I inserted a session on chakras under my own initiative. Using a borrowed dowsing pendulum and (it has to be admitted) with a good deal of trepidation and doubt, I asked for two volunteers who knew little or nothing about chakras. My two volunteers (one lying on the floor and the other holding the pendulum) were soon able to identify the seven major chakras without any prompting from me. Further, we established two facts often ignored in chakra literature, firstly that alternate chakras rotate in opposing directions and secondly, there are a number of secondary or minor chakras, including one in the palm of the hand.

I was now much more confident about talking about (and researching) this elusive subject, which in the wrong hands can sound distinctly like "mumbo-jumbo". I started to discuss it in various yoga day seminars I was running (and indeed, still do). Each time a seminar came along, I seemed to make a new discovery. Three were particularly important. The first was that men and women have opposing and complementary chakra systems. The second was that if we change the hand holding the pendulum from right to left (or vice-versa), we reverse the rotation of the pendulum, demonstrating that the movement is caused by an interaction between two organisms and is not fixed immutably, in the way the position of an organ is fixed. The third is that the behaviour of the chakras can reveal mood and health. One lady (not known to me personally) who was attending one of my seminars seemed desperate to be the "body on the floor". When another student (who was known to me) held the pendulum over the first (perineal or root) chakra, nothing happened. Embarrassing failure seemed to loom. I told my student to try the next (sacral) chakra. Again, nothing. Just as I was about to ask for another volunteer, the pendulum started to move, albeit reluctantly. Instead of the steady, circular motion normally seen, it swung awkwardly, diagonally across the body. At this point, to everyone's astonishment, the "body on the floor" volunteered the information that she was awaiting an operation "down there" and wanted her condition confirmed by her chakra status. This was the evidence I was looking for – evidence of practical, diagnostic use. Evidence of direct, therapeutic benefit came later. Sadly, my subject had to leave early and I was unable to keep in contact to offer any further assistance. On another occasion, I was holding the pendulum personally. The first three chakras responded normally. The fourth (heart) chakra responded by swinging wildly. My subject was a young, attractive woman in her twenties. It doesn't take a genius to work out that the heart chakra has strong emotional connections to feelings of unconditional love. I jokingly remarked that there must be a wonderful man in her life, whereupon the pendulum stopped and reversed! Clearly, her feelings about the mystery man (woman?) were confused. I had no wish to embarrass her in a group situation, so refrained from questioning her further but the demonstration was certainly revealing.

So far, so good. I had evidence of diagnostic possibilities, which could easily be interpreted intuitively with a little experience. However, I had no idea how to correct imbalanced or sluggish chakras, other than suggesting certain yoga postures and other practices – not much use to a non-yogi! Further, people with out of balance energy systems are often highly resistant to yoga or indeed, exercise in general. The remark "why don't you take up yoga" is often unhelpful. The "what can *you* do for *me*?" mindset seems to prevail over the "what can I do *for myself*" attitude of the practicing yogi.

Once again, the idea of chakras as a therapeutic tool slipped to the back of my mind, as I carried on with my day-to-day life as a full-time yoga teacher, writer, researcher and occasional hypnotherapist. In the summer of 2009, I was on holiday with my partner Diane, who is a practicing kinesiologist. We were staying in Glastonbury UK, which has a well-deserved reputation for being an inspirational sort of place, much favoured by mystics, visionaries and working therapists. Tired after a long journey, I quickly fell asleep, only to wake up in the early hours with the correct method of stimulating a sluggish chakra fully formed in my imagination. The power of the subconscious! This was a delightful surprise and inspired a shopping spree in the local bookshops and later at home online. I was soon able to confirm what I had long suspected, namely that a lot of the information on chakras "out there" was ill-informed guesswork and the product of what I call "cut and paste thinking".

What do I mean by "cut and paste thinking"? We are all guilty occasionally. We read or are told an idea or concept that strikes an emotional chord. We fail to qualify or question its assumptions, especially if the source appears to be authoritative. Then we pass it on to others, either intact or imbedded into other ideas. Quite often, our thinking becomes a string of associated, preconceived ideas or prejudices, which have their origins inside someone else's mind. Just as the viral e-mail spreads around the globe, so do errors and illusions. Eternal doubt and debate is the price of intellectual freedom. At the risk of seeming arrogant, I would ask my readers to try to put aside, or at least question, much of what they have heard or read about chakras and life energy. However, I must add that I do not profess to be the final authority – there isn't one. Further, although I feel I can reasonably claim to have a bit of a knack at reading and interpreting chakras, I absolutely do *not* claim to have any special, psychic or supernatural ability. What we are discussing and investigating is an entirely natural, though poorly understood phenomenon. Like psychology, "chakrology" is an imprecise science. However, in its defence, I must add that the techniques in this book are evidence based, even though there is little hard science. Nothing has been accepted at face value, without personal experience, unless a clear statement to that effect is made.

The techniques require little training or practice to master and almost no special equipment. A treatment couch is useful but not essential and a duvet or sleeping bag to lie on if you are using the floor and a dowsing pendulum, which is a crystal or piece of shaped mineral on the end of a short chain. They are available from new age, crystal and gemstone retailers for a modest outlay. Personal qualifications? A fairly steady hand, an open mind and a reasonably lively energy system are called for. Mapping and balancing the chakras is not for the severely debilitated or for those with closed minds – even if that mind is in favour of the concept. Everything else, we can learn. When we have mastered the technique, we can use it as a "stand alone" therapy or in conjunction with other therapies. As we shall see, some (but not all) of the techniques can be used as "DIY therapy".

A word of warning, though - If you are ill, or think you may be, get a proper medical diagnosis from a trained practitioner, which usually means your own GP. This is a sensible precaution, even if you opt later for the "complementary route" or – increasingly popular these days – a combination of orthodox and complementary. This observation applies both to the would-be therapist and the client.

2. UNDERSTANDING LIFE ENERGY

If we fail to grasp and understand the concept of life energy, we fail to understand the chakras. It is a subject bedevilled by misunderstanding, distortion, downright dottiness and, above all, implacable (and irrational) hostility on the part of the scientific "establishment". Once again I must point out the poor quality of much of the so-called information "out there". Sadly, much of this misinformation comes from people who should know better, such as writers of science and complementary medicine books. I hope to put the record straight as succinctly as I can, without being too doctrinaire, for it is a subject that urgently requires further sensible, open-minded research. Such research requires funding and that is, at present, conspicuous by its absence. It is mainly the pursuit of enthusiastic amateurs and professional scientists who earn their living in other, more academically respectable fields.

The theory has probably been around since the Stone Age. It is quite simply this. *There exists all around us and within us a largely invisible but potent energy, which animates all living things.* Further extensions of this theory argue that it animates the entire universe, including the non-living but that assertion is beyond the remit of this book. We are not discussing cosmology, only one inhabitant of the universe, with occasional references to other inhabitants. The name varies according to cultural and linguistic standpoint. Prana, qi, ki, sen, od, orgone and vis naturalis are a few of the many names. As I am approaching the subject largely from a yogic perspective, I shall mainly use the term *prana* – a Sanskrit word meaning "life force". It also means "breath" and this dual meaning is, as we shall see, highly significant.

We must ask the question "what evidence is there for such a force?" There is, in fact, rather a lot. Some of it is incontrovertible, though ignored by science and the media. *Subjective* evidence of an internal, personal life energy is easy to come by. Try this simple exercise.

- Lie on the floor with the legs straight and the arms alongside the body, palms upwards. Close your eyes. (This is known in yoga as *Savasana*).
- Deepen your breathing.
- Contract the right buttock, so that the pelvis tilts slightly to the left.
- Release the right buttock and immediately contract the left, tilting the pelvis to the right.
- Keep going from right to left and back again, at least 50 times. Keep breathing slowly and deeply. Get into a natural rhythm and speed. Let go - surrender to the movement.
- After 50-100 cycles, stop and observe how you feel. You should feel a curious "fizzing" sensation through most of the body. This is your personal life energy at work. The more expansive the feeling, the healthier your energy system.
- This is an excellent exercise to do on a regular basis, to improve health and vitality.

Independent evidence is more difficult but not impossible to find. To be sure of your ground, ask someone else who you know well how they react *physically* to a strong emotional experience, such as great music, a moving or scary programme on TV or a sporting "high" or "low". Ask yourself the same question. You will get comments such as "the hair stood up on the back of my neck" "I got goose bumps" "I got a sinking feeling in the pit of my stomach" "I got a lovely, warm feeling" "I went weak at the knees" "my heart missed a beat" "I came out in a cold sweat" etc. Clearly, a *tangible physical force* is at work here, otherwise we would feel nothing. The usual named suspect is electricity. These feelings are the result of electrical activity in the nerve cells, we are told. This is a plausible but entirely erroneous explanation. There is indeed electrical activity in the nervous system, indeed, throughout the body. However, I (and others more highly qualified) have measured the electrical potential of my own skin (and the mouth, which is much more sensitive and moist) at around 4-5 millivolts. A millivolt is one thousandth of a volt and a single cell battery delivers about 1.5 volts, i.e. 1500 millivolts, to get things into perspective. These potentials are far too low to be perceived by the body's nervous system. The highly sensitive tongue will perceive a potential of about 1 volt. Something else is causing us to perceive these emotional forces physically. That "something" is our own life energy, which we best perceive when it is on the move, hence our expression "it was moving", to describe a deep emotional experience.

Subjective evidence of an external energy field around the body, sometimes called the aura can also be found but not always "to order". A lot depends on the subject, the observer and the conditions. It does not show up very often in photographs without special enhancement. However, try this simple experiment, which like the first, requires no special equipment.

- Ask a friend to stand in front of a grainy background. Brown is a good colour but almost anything may work if this is unavailable.
- Ask them to breathe slowly and deeply.
- Relax your eyes and try to look "past" the head and shoulders.
- If you are perceptive, you may see a faint, mist-like emanation, with a clear band about 1-3" wide between the aura and the body.
- Don't be disheartened if you see nothing – if you do not have a trained eye or a certain degree of natural talent, you may not be able to.

Subjective evidence for an external life energy in the atmosphere can also be easily found but again, not "to order" –

- On a bright, sunny day, look up at the sky, away from the sun.
- Relax the eyes and pause.
- After a few seconds or maybe a minute, you should see white spinning dots, moving in a spiral or serpentine form. You may also see faint, pulsating grey patches, though this is less easily seen.
- On a cloudy day, look at the base of a cloud. You will see the very same white spinning dots. The grey patches are not normally visible in cloudy weather.

You need to be by the sea or a large lake for this one –

- On a bright, sunny day, relax the eyes and look *just above* the surface of the water. In theory, you should see nothing at all. In fact -
- You may be able to observe a shimmering and streaming effect. The streaming effect may not be in the same direction as the wind.
- It may help to look at a localised patch through a tube.
- This is the atmospheric life energy. Its discoverer called it "orgone".

Objective evidence of life energy requires special equipment, though it is not beyond the reach of the real enthusiast. The *Life Energy (LE) Meter* was invented by David Marett of *Heliognosis*. It does not measure life energy in absolute terms, in the way a volt meter can measure my mains voltage at home, since no such absolute scale exists at present. It measures the percentage increase or decrease against background levels. I possess one of these meters, which is something of a "show stopper" at day seminars and training sessions. Plate 1 shows the meter at zero and plate 2 the effect of my palm near the plate electrode. A fresh cutting from a vigorous climber in the author's garden (plate 3) has a similar, though less pronounced, effect, but as it dies off the effect diminishes. A source of electromagnetic energy, such as a mobile phone, has a zero effect, whether on standby, ring or talk mode. A great deal of useful research can be done with this item, though it is certainly not essential equipment for the aspiring "chakrologist", who needs very little in the way of equipment.

I have gone into some detail about these phenomena, at risk of boring my reader, in order to counter a common illusion, namely that prana is merely a metaphysical, cultural, religious or philosophical concept – a spiritual, rather than a real energy. It is nothing of the sort. If it were, we would be unable to harness it for anything useful and the activities of many complementary practitioners would be ineffective. "It's all in the mind" is the parrot cry of the sceptic. We have all heard of the placebo effect and the "miracle cures" that have been brought about by inert, dummy "medications". I have news for such sceptics. You may be able to fool me with a pink aspirin but you can't fool a plant or an experimental mouse. Once again, I must beg the indulgence of my reader, who is unlikely to be aware of the details of this fascinating and important work.

Plate 1.
LE Meter set to zero, showing wooden plate electrode on the left.

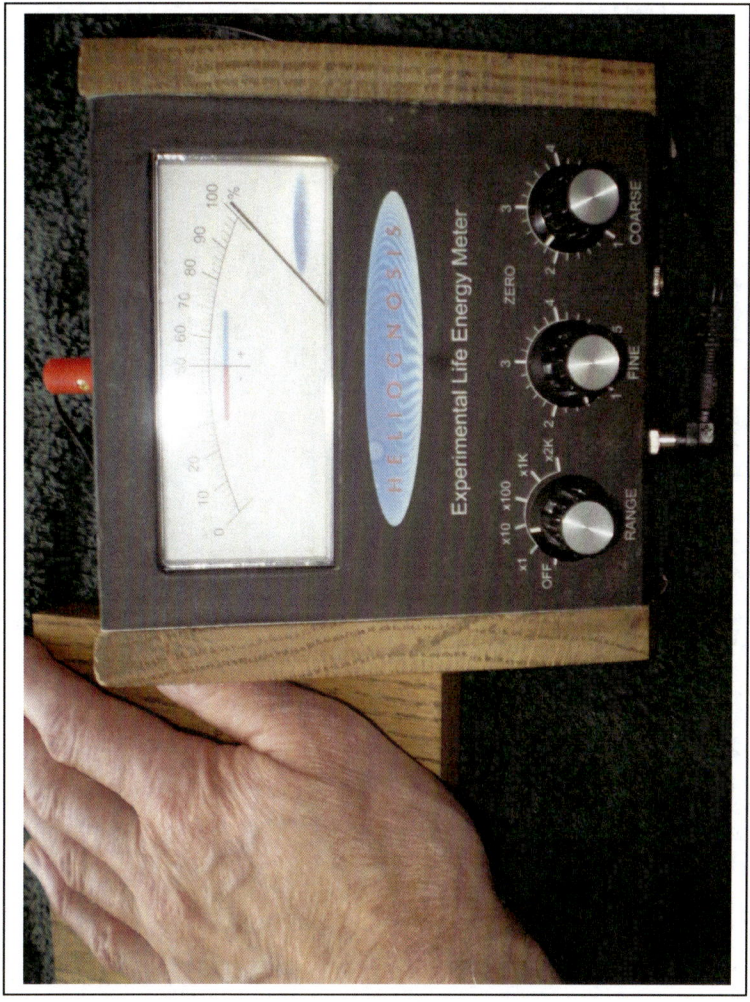

Plate 2 –

LE meter needle deflected to 100% by the author's hand.

Plate 3 –

LE meter with needle deflected by a shrub cutting.

I must now condense my material considerably to avoid distorting the nature of my subject matter of chakras and fly off on a tangent. I would draw readers' attention to my source material (which I strongly recommend) if they wish to know more. Wilhelm Reich started his career as a doctor and orthodox Freudian psychoanalyst in the early 1920s. Freud and Reich later fell out but that's another story. Impatient with the slow and unreliable results he was getting, Reich developed a "bodymind" therapy, treating the whole person. Even his detractors (there are many, who usually haven't bothered to read his books, let alone attempt the experiments) grudgingly admit to his brilliant pioneering work in this field. WR is the unsung "Granddaddy" of most of the modern bodymind therapies, such as Rolfing, Feldenkrais etc and some psychotherapy techniques, such as Gestalt.

When his patients underwent an emotional release, he (and his patients) noticed an energy movement in the body. Streaming, bubbling and crawling sensations were reported. What was the nature of this energy? Initially, WR suspected electricity and even coined the term "bioelectricity". Using volunteer experimental subjects, he soon established that, as discussed above, this was not the case. The electrical potentials found were far too low. The experiment did, however, prove one positive, namely the antithesis of anxiety and sexuality[1].

By a long and circuitous route, involving occasional accidental observations, he established that there was a mysterious "something" animating all living things, including humans and the very small, which he observed and filmed over a long period of time, using a high quality microscope[2]. He was one of the first scientists to use time-lapse microphotography. He called this "something" orgone energy and its study, orgonomy. Soon after, he established that this energy was in the atmosphere all around us and

---

[1] Reich, W. *The Bioelectrical Investigation of Sexuality and Anxiety.* Farrah, Strauss and Giroux.
[2] Reich, W. *The Bion Experiments on the Origin of Life.* Farrah, Strauss and Giroux.

could be amplified in a specially constructed cabinet he called the orgone energy accumulator, abbreviated to "orac". It is a very simple and logical step of the imagination to identify "orgone" with "prana" and "prana" with "life energy". The phenomenon is the same, only the name varies, though "orgone" is perhaps a more scientific concept and label.

It is the orac that we can use to prove objectively that the life energy exists. It has to be cheerfully admitted that it looks like a rather improbable device. It has no *apparent* external energy connection, such as a mains lead. Further, it has been the subject of much prurient and wildly inaccurate speculation, being dubbed a "sex box" or "orgasm box". It is nothing of the sort and was never claimed to be. I can report from personal experience that sadly, it has only a marginal effect on sexual potency. If you're looking for a sex aid, it's back to the drawing board, I'm afraid.

An orac can be constructed by anyone with reasonable DIY skills. I have two – one large enough to sit in and another smaller, research version. WR used experimental cancer mice (and later, human patients) to achieve remarkable results in tumour reduction. Such experiments might today be impossible outside orthodox medical research for ethical and practical reasons. However, we can use seeds and many researchers (including my brother Peter) have achieved accelerated germination and growth using a wide variety of species[1]. I have successfully tried the same experiment myself, using dwarf beans. A tray or pot of seeds is placed in the orac and a control tray or pot is left nearby, in a box or similar light-proof container, so that conditions are otherwise identical. The experimental tray in the orac always germinates first and has more vigorous growth.

As I see it, this proves conclusively that the life force exists and can be harnessed for practical purposes. With seeds, there can be no question of the influence of suggestion,

---

[1] Jones, P. *A Seed Germination Experiment with the Orgone Accumulator.* CORE. www.orgonomyuk.org.uk

which tends to bedevil experiments on humans. Many other successful experiments have been carried out over the years since Reich's death with almost zero coverage by the media. Many have been carried out by professional, qualified scientists often working in their spare time and almost always self-financed. It would be possible to fill a book with details but I must now return to my principal subject.

3. MYTH AND MAGIC

Yoga (and its attendant theory and philosophy) is a very ancient practice. Five millennia would be a conservative estimate. In prescientific cultures, there is little concept of energy as we know it today through physics. Such cultures therefore rely on the potency of myth to explain such phenomena. Early man would certainly be intuitively aware of *prana* but would have called it spirit, rather than energy. We know this because he left exquisite "energy signatures" on his artwork, such as carved bones and stonework. The famous "passage grave", (which is really a temple) at Newgrange, Ireland is one magnificent example of many in Europe. I use the term "man" but maybe I should have written "woman", as these societies seem to have been much less patriarchal than those that came later.[1] So the early yogis would have equated prana with "spirit" rather than "energy" but the reality was the same. Prana is mentioned in the Vedas, a very ancient oral tradition, which Hindus claim to be seven thousand years old. In Europe and elsewhere, under the baleful influence of life-denying desert religions, the concept of prana faded (though never quite disappeared) from intellectual consciousness. This did not happen in the East for subtle and complex social reasons. Putting it rather simplistically, Eastern thought is "evolutionist", Western thought is "revolutionist".

What do I mean by those terms? In the West, new ideas tend to supplant the old, often in a violent upheaval. The Reformation was a good example. In the East, ancient wisdom and ideas are deeply respected and not jettisoned so easily. The new is simply grafted on to the old, even when it is sometimes almost contradictory – to the occasional despair of Westerners trying to make sense of it all. So, the advance of Western ideas and science in the East has not led to wholesale destruction of old ideas about prana. The West has a different tale to tell. With the triumph of scientific materialism in the nineteenth century, old ideas about a life-energy and the origins of life slowly fell

---

[1] Gimbutas, M. *The Language of the Goddess.*

out of favour until eventually they became the subject of considerable hostility and even ridicule. Evidence in favour was ignored as a type of flat-earth theory and evidence against, no matter how flimsy, was seized upon avidly. Interestingly, Darwin's theory of evolution was distinctly revolutionist, a paradox the man himself would probably have enjoyed. Incidentally, Darwin made no comment at all about a life-energy and hedged his bets about the actual origins of life (as opposed to the origin of species). Opponents of the idea will look to the great man in vain. Eventually, hostility to the prana concept became so bitter in the West that it culminated in marginalisation, persecution and book burning. We are not just talking now about Nazi Germany, but good ol' USA and even civilised and democratic Norway.

The "flip-side" of revolutionist/mechanistic thinking is mysticism. Thoughtful people often turn to mysticism (either the Eastern or Western variety) as a reaction to the excesses of scientific materialism. "What has science brought us?" they will ask. "Nuclear weapons, pollution, global warming and a cynical culture of disbelief – and they can't even fix a runny nose". They have a point, even though that point is a little unfair. Let me explain why I feel we should resist the temptation to turn to mysticism when studying our subject.

Mysticism is difficult to define. My dictionary defines a mystic as "a person who seeks by contemplation and self-surrender to obtain unity or identity with or absorption into the Deity or the ultimate reality, or who believes in the spiritual apprehension of truths that are beyond the understanding". This seems as good a definition as any. I did plenty of contemplation (and meditation) in order to understand the chakras and prana. So I'm not too upset if someone calls me a mystic. Mysticism of this type is one of several valid thinking modes we need to function creatively, without disabling pessimism or cynicism. This is the type I call *functional* or *poetic mysticism*. However, we can get locked into mysticism, as some do without even realising. It takes over their entire psychological structure, causing a type of emotional and psychological disablement. This is the downside I call *structural mysticism*. When mysticism evolves into organised religion, it usually becomes patriarchal, renunciate and life denying. It can (and often does) distort rational thinking. One man who called me with serious health problems would only agree to have his chakras balanced if I employed the angels he had been communing with. He would not even agree to the free consultation I offered him. I never heard from him again.

Now a belief in angels is fine by me. A youthful William Blake "saw" angels in a tree. His mysticism inspired some of the finest and most radical poetry in the English Language. Some of the greatest artworks created by humanity have been inspired by mysticism. Mystics often attain a radiant contentment and love that is often denied to the non-mystic. I sometimes use the image of an angel or deity as a metaphor myself but if we convince ourselves that they are a concrete reality and the only route to salvation, we are limiting our lives intolerably. We cannot harness prana and chakras if they are "beyond understanding". Indeed, anything that is "beyond understanding" is, by definition, beyond practical use.

Kundalini is an ancient myth that needs an explanation before we move on to pranic anatomy and its practical "nuts and bolts". The serpent is an image that is often used in pre-scientific cultures as a metaphor for prana. It is significant that, in modern Western and middle-eastern cultures, the serpent is considered sinister. It seduced Eve. In Indian and ancient, prehistoric European cultures, it is considered holy. Kundalini means "she who is coiled" and the myth tells us that she is coiled round the base of the spine three and a half times. She can be thought of as the Goddess within. When she is wakened by intense yoga practice, she rushes up the spine, pierces the chakras and triggers enlightenment. Kundalini, therefore is almost synonymous with prana but not quite. Sleeping, she symbolises *potential* rather than *actual, flowing* prana. Fully awakening Kundalini is the work of a lifetime for the dedicated yogi and need not concern us here. Thinking mythically and metaphorically, we could say that we are giving her a gentle nudge and arousing her from her slumbers. We are concerned more with helping the sick and troubled. We are not using magic (though it may sometimes seem that we do) – we are using a perfectly natural, though poorly understood phenomenon.

4. PRANIC ANATOMY

Because prana is mass free and not electromagnetic in its fundamental nature, its flowing manifestation could be described as pre-cellular. Its movements do not correspond with any known organs in the body. Therefore references to fixed body parts should be regarded only as external signposts, not addresses. Further, there is ample evidence that the position of each chakra tends to vary a little between individuals and probably according to the emotional state of that individual. There are also some variations of opinion amongst writers about some locations. These are important points to bear in mind when trying to locate the chakras.

Nadis are energy channels in the living organism. They differ from the meridians familiar to practitioners of Traditional Chinese Medicine and its offshoots in that they are in the core of the body, whereas meridians are mainly on the periphery, hence their easy access by a trained professional using needles or gentle pressure. The model I am about to outline is unproven but fits the known facts that I have been able to ascertain using human volunteers and a mapping technique that I shall outline shortly. It may seem improbable to some but I can only report what I have seen in front of witnesses and what I have seen others able to do with no prior knowledge of chakras and their positions or behaviour at all. There are three principal nadis and very many subsidiary ones, which need not concern us here. I must emphasise that figure 1 is a *theoretical schematic* – we shall probably never know the exact routes of the nadis, as they are invisible. Further, the chakras are not evenly spaced out as they are in the diagram. Nature is seldom that obliging! The numbering and English names are my own, though some have been used by other writers. The traditional Sanskrit names are in italics.

Figure 1 – A schematic diagram of the nadis.

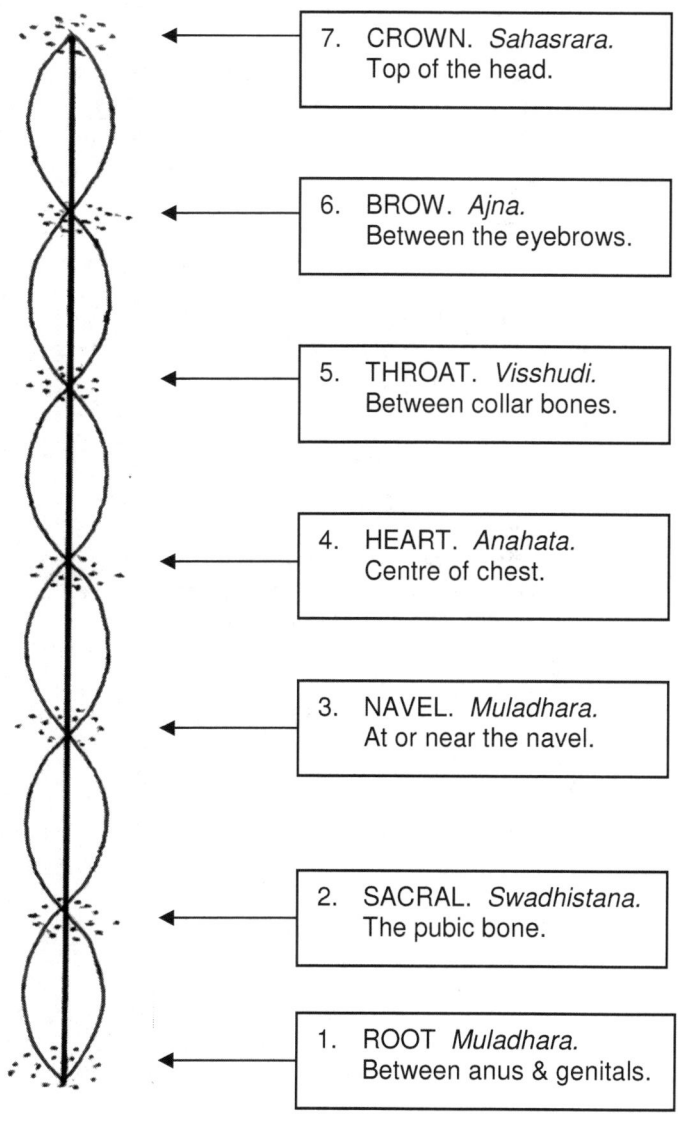

7. CROWN. *Sahasrara.*
   Top of the head.

6. BROW. *Ajna.*
   Between the eyebrows.

5. THROAT. *Visshudi.*
   Between collar bones.

4. HEART. *Anahata.*
   Centre of chest.

3. NAVEL. *Muladhara.*
   At or near the navel.

2. SACRAL. *Swadhistana.*
   The pubic bone.

1. ROOT *Muladhara.*
   Between anus & genitals.

Sushumna runs up the centre of the body from the base of the spine to the brain. Some say it is identical to the spinal chord but in my opinion, it lies in front of, and independent of, the spinal column. It is represented by the thicker central line. In reality, it is unlikely that line would be perfectly straight. Again, nature doesn't do straight lines! According to yogic theory, Sushumna lies dormant until we have achieved enlightenment – usually a lifetime's work. My personal opinion is that Sushumna is not quite as dormant as we would believe.

Ida and Pingala are two nadis that twine around Sushumna in a double helix, similar to the well-known DNA model. Where they cross in the core of the body, there is an energy hotspot or vortex which we call a *chakra*. These are indicated by the dotted spirals. Each chakra seat or centre is in the core of the body but all the major chakras also manifest a tangible (and therefore usable) force outside the body. The body's periphery should be thought of as "prana transparent". As Ida and Pingala spiral up the body, their directions of approach towards each other are reversing, so it follows that the rotation of the chakras reverses as we move up the body. Repeated practical mapping demonstrations show that this in fact the case. In addition to the seven major chakras, there are a number of minor chakras, which are also capable of external manifestation, though usually less strongly. They appear to be located closer to the body periphery than the major chakras. So far, our information falls within the confines of traditional yoga teaching.

I am reluctant to claim credit for what follows as many yogis do research under a cloak of anonymity and much knowledge is very ancient and its sources are lost. However, I would ask my reader to look once again at my theoretical diagram. As the nadis spiral away from the central S*ushumna*, they approach the periphery of the body. This is where we would expect to find a lesser "hotspot" or minor chakra. This is again what we find using mapping techniques. The minor chakras are mainly off-centre or *bilateral*, to use the anatomical terminology and roughly on an imaginary line drawn horizontally between principal chakras.

For example, between the brow and throat chakras, either side we find a minor chakra behind the ear lobe. The major chakras manifest in the front (anterior) of the body and in the back (posterior) of the body, except the root and crown, which only have one manifestation, due to their position. Sushumna is the axis of each major chakra. As it is not necessarily exactly vertical (in the standing position), the posterior manifestation may not be exactly in line with the anterior manifestation but they are close enough to find, once we are familiar with the anterior position. As the spinning vortex of prana breaks through the periphery (the skin), it comes into direct contact with the atmospheric prana, setting up a secondary vortex with a roughly horizontal axis. Again, we are talking about a standing position. In a treatment scenario, the client would normally be lying down, so the external axis would be roughly vertical. It is this external vortex we use to locate and balance the chakras.

The limbs call for further consideration. We do not yet know the exact route of the pranic flow but it is almost certainly mainly through the second (sacral) chakra for the legs and the fifth (throat) for the arms, with additional supplementary routes through the first (root) and fourth (heart). The limbs house important minor chakras but no major ones, as far as we can tell. When I started my research, I was able to quickly find one on the palm of each hand, which were very useful for demonstration purposes and no doubt help to explain the effectiveness of intuitive "hands on" healing. Interestingly, the left hand chakra vortex is the opposite direction to the right hand, and the male right hand is contrary to the female right hand. This also applies to the principal chakras, hence my earlier assertion that the male and female pranic systems exactly complement each other – food for thought for the gender warriors! Incidentally, the contrary energy systems of male and female reinforces my long-held view that sex is not just about genitals and hormones, it is about something much more profound, deeply ingrained in our very nature as living organisms. "If there is a chakra on each palm", I reasoned "there must be one on the sole of each foot". Indeed there was. I was also able to locate one on the crease of the elbows and knees and the shoulders, hips and pelvis. My final pair of "minors" I shall call "intercostals". They are situated near the bottom of the ribcage, on the side (lateral line) of the body. They are rather more difficult to locate. Finally, we must bear in mind two (possibly more) remarkable phenomena, namely out of body chakras, one about a foot above the head and another about a foot below the feet, which is obviously only detectable in a lying position. The former is sometimes called the "heaven star" and the latter the "earth star". So far, I have been unable to find much practical use for these two but who knows? Our research is still in its infancy. Some may feel the assertion in this paragraph improbable to the point of being ridiculous but once again, I can only report that which I have carefully investigated. Some writers have asserted that there are many more out of body chakras but I have been unable to find them, using my preferred technique. I look forward to being found wrong!

Once again, I must stress that all this is not the final word and is at variance with the views of some writers. John Cross, whose views and clinical experience I greatly respect, has identified a joker in the pack, namely a spleen chakra, situated above and to the left of the navel, which is neither central nor bilateral. I have resisted the temptation to indulge in cut and paste thinking and can only stress that I have been unable to find such a chakra. (One of my students has done, however). This most definitely does not mean that I do not believe it exists or has clinical use – it may simply be too weak to show up using my technique – or maybe it is simply a very significant point, rather than a chakra. The body has many such peripheral points, known as acupoints or tsubos. They could, perhaps be called "mini-chakras". The location of chakras two (sacral) and three (navel) is especially prone to variation. Some writers have the second chakra much higher, about midway between the perineum and the navel and the navel chakra also higher and called the solar plexus chakra. John Cross also has a pair of secondary chakras either side of the physical navel. Again, I have been unable to find these with my technique. To complicate the issue still further, the Swamis of the Bihar School of Yoga, whose views and very considerable knowledge I also greatly respect, have the female root chakra higher than the male, near the cervix. This has not been my experience, using both male and female subjects. The likely reason for much of this variation has already been stated, namely that there is almost certainly some positional and axis variation from person to person. There also appears to be more variation in the positions of chakras than in the positions of acupoints, reinforcing my view (and that of tradition) that the principal nadis are in the core of the body and the meridians (mainly) on the periphery. Despite all this uncertainty, once we have mapped our client's principal chakras, we have enough reasonably firm ground to proceed with our practical work.

5. PRACTICAL PRELIMINARIES.

Figure 2 - Approximate location of the major chakras.

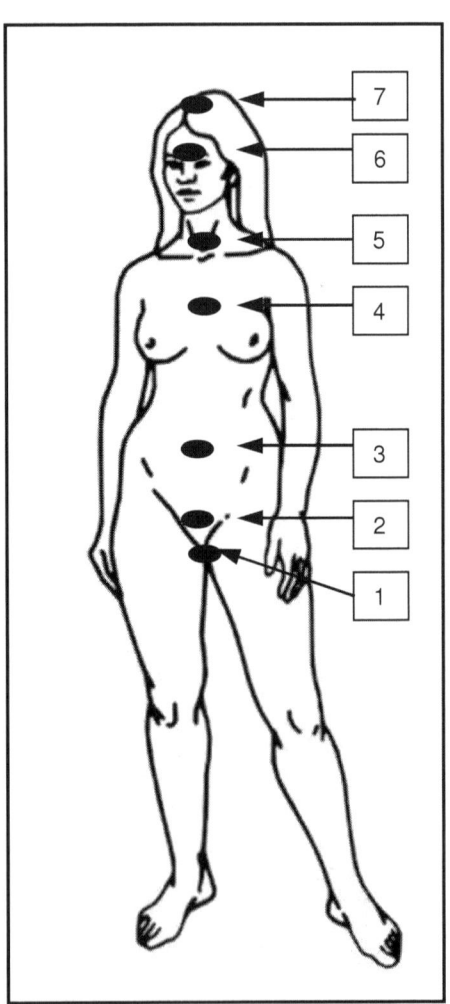

NB. Major chakras manifest at the front and back of the body.

Minor chakras are located bilaterally and usually manifest only on the front or the back of the body, so the knee chakra is found on the back of the physical joint and the shoulder is found on the front.

Take a good look at figure 2. In theory, you don't have to know the chakra locations as you can find them using the mapping technique I am about to describe. In practice, it saves a great deal of frustrating and time consuming error if you at least know roughly where they are and how they should behave.

Now try the following simple mapping exercise. You will need a friend as a guinea-pig and a dowsing pendulum. There is absolutely no need for the friend to undress.

A reminder that a dowsing pendulum is a piece of crystal or mineral on the end of a short chain around 20 cm long with a bead at the other end. It is your only piece of essential equipment. They are available from new age, crystal and gemstone retailers. There is absolutely no evidence that the expensive versions using rare crystals work any better than the cheaper versions, though obviously aesthetics may also influence your choice. Some of the coloured crystals can be very beautiful and lift the spirit almost at a glance. An important point to bear in mind - the pendulum is a highly effective but slightly blunt instrument. It cannot pick up relatively small deficiencies and imbalances. Further, much depends on the skill, experience and vitality of the therapist, hence the need to balance all the chakras, regardless of what the pendulum indicates. Obviously, we spend longer on any that appear to be "out". Don't try to map your own chakras without assistance - it can't be done.

- Ask your friend to hold out their right hand, palm upwards.
- Using your dominant hand (right if you are right handed), suspend the pendulum over the palm with the point about 10-12 cm (4-5 inches) above the palm. Hold it as steadily as you can. Don't try to cheat!
- Allow the end of the pendulum to stabilise, and then wait a few seconds.
- After a few seconds, the weight should start to slowly swing, in a circular motion. It is almost impossible to fake this motion convincingly by moving the hand.
- Make a note of the direction of swing i.e. clockwise or anticlockwise.
- Now repeat the exercise, using your friend's left hand. You should find that it swings in the opposite direction.
- Now try the same thing, only using your non-dominant hand (left if you are right handed).
- You should find that the results are the exact reverse.
- You are observing the energetic interaction of two organisms, your own and your friend's. Don't forget, you too have a hand chakra!
- If you have a second friend of the opposite sex, you can repeat the exercise. You will find that their direction of swing is the exact opposite.

Now, try the following exercise, which astonished me, when I first tried it. It was done very much on a whim, without expectation of any result. It can be done without any assistance.

- Take a fresh apple and place it on a table or work surface, stalk or stalk end upwards.
- Hold the pendulum with the point about 2-3 cm (1-1.5 inches) above the apple.
- Wait a few seconds.
- The pendulum will start to swing, though less vigorously than with the human hand.
- Remove the stalk if it has one and turn the apple over.
- Using the same hand, repeat the above. The pendulum will swing in the opposite direction.
- Try the same thing, using the growth point of a reasonably vigorous plant. The same thing will happen.
- If you have some fairly fresh, healthy looking cut flowers at home, try again, using a flower. Once again, the same thing will happen.

If you have a pet, that is not too excitable, try the same thing. Our household is not blessed with pets, so I am unable to try this experiment but I suspect you will find that cats, dogs and other quadrupeds have multiple chakras but not as many as humans. A yoga colleague counted five on his dog but I have been unable to confirm his findings. One of my students was unable to find any on her family pet. What you have now established in your own mind is the deeply rooted nature of chakras and life energy. They are not just a human phenomenon, they are universal. What we have witnessed is the tangible, kinetic effect of prana. We are now ready to move on a stage.

6. MAPPING AND STIMULATING

We are now ready to map and, if necessary, treat the major chakras. A few points need to be borne in mind. Firstly, the size and vitality of the external energy field varies according to vitality, mood etc and the same applies to your ability to map it. Secondly, the energy field widens as we move up the body, then tapers again, so we need to hold the pendulum rather closer at the lower chakras (one and two) and the upper chakras (five, six and seven) than we do in the middle chakras (three and four). Your friend or client should be lying supine (flat on the back), with the feet a little apart. The knees can be bent for comfort if necessary. Again, there is no need to undress, though thick, heavy clothing is a bad idea.

Ask your client to deepen their breath a little, without forcing. Do the same yourself. This stimulates the pranic anatomy a little and assists observation. Using your dominant hand, hold the point of your pendulum about 2-3 inches above the crotch. Wait for the pendulum to start to move. This may take ten or more seconds. Observe the direction and nature of the swing. Write down briefly what you observe. It might read "One - clockwise, sluggish" or some such. Now, move the pendulum up about 4-5 inches (10-12 cm). It should swing in the opposite direction but may not if there is a problem. Making notes as you go, move up the chakras in succession. Chakras are normally numbered from the root, so the sacral is two, navel three and so on. However, bear in mind that if you have read about chakras elsewhere, the writer may have numbered them from the crown or even at random. As you move up the body, the direction should reverse each time. If it fails to reverse, or (more commonly) hardly moves or trembles rather than swings, there is a problem. However, we must also remember once again that the pendulum is a blunt instrument. Its behaviour should be considered as a rough guide, which requires interpretation, rather than precise information.

The problem is almost certainly that the chakra is sluggish or constricted and needs stimulating. This is quite easy to do:–

First, work out which direction the pendulum *should* have swung, by comparing it to its neighbours. Let us say, for example, that it should have swung clockwise but is actually swinging anticlockwise or just trembling. Hold the open, dominant hand (the one you have been using all along) palm downwards over the suspect chakra without the pendulum. The distance from the body will vary according to the chakra location and the vitality of the client but if in doubt, about 12-18 inches (30-45 cm) should be fine. Pause for a moment. Now start to *slowly* circle the palm around the vertical axis of the chakra, in the *correct* direction. As you do so, *slowly* bring the hand towards the body and reduce the diameter of the circle, so your palm is moving in a downward spiral. As your hand approaches the body, allow your fingers to curl downwards a little, then place the index, middle and ring fingers, bunched together onto the surface of the body, pressing lightly. Continue with light, very small circling movements, always in the same direction.

The whole exercise is unlikely to take more than a minute. Pause for a moment, then map the chakra again. It should have corrected itself. If not, repeat the exercise, with slightly more (but never excessive) pressure at the end. Another excellent method of stimulation is rhythmic gentle tapping with the index, middle or ring finger, about 2 to 3 taps per second for 20-30 seconds. This requires direct body contact or very lightweight clothing. If there is still no progress, try the back (posterior) aspect of the body but remember that you need to reverse the direction of your circling. Finally, remap all seven chakras to check that everything is OK.

Once we have mastered the mapping and stimulating technique described above, we are well on the way to mastering the art of chakra therapy. Further, we have thoroughly acquainted ourselves with the major chakras and their behaviour. We are ready to look at chakra balancing.

7. BALANCING

Figure 3 - Major and minor chakras.

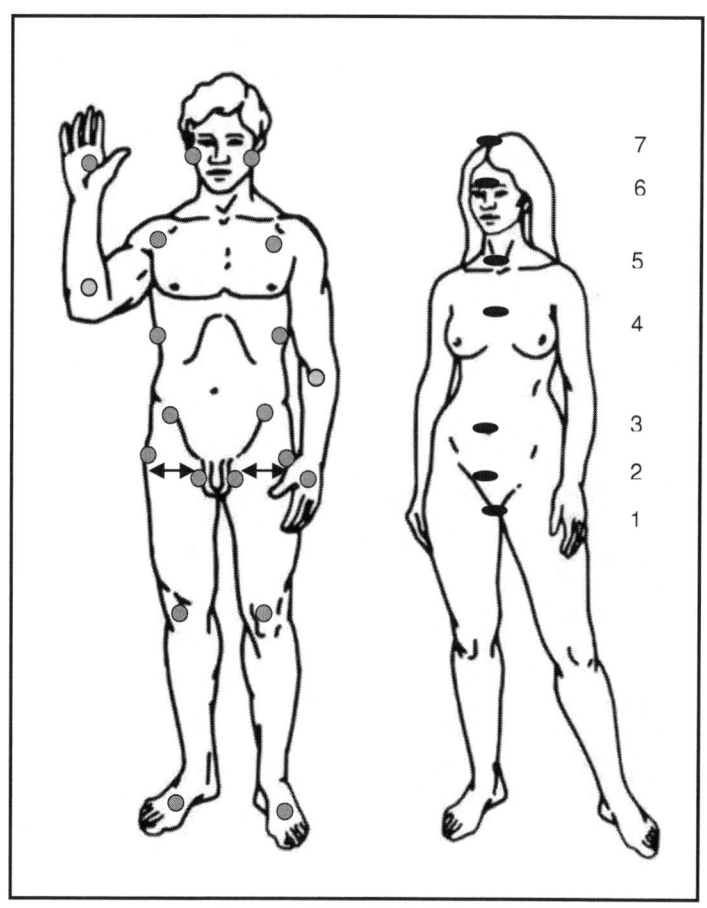

We have now reached the core of our therapeutic technique. Chakra balancing is a little more complex than mapping and stimulating from the technical standpoint but eminently practical and understandable with a little practice. We need to have a mental picture of the locations of the minor chakras, which we will use extensively. We will only use those whose existence I have been able to confirm, so there may well be some variance between my technique and that of other writers, although the basic principles will be the same.

Study the chakra diagrams (figure 3) carefully. You will notice that the female figure is the same as figure 2. It shows the seven major chakras. For the sake of clarity, the minor chakras are shown separately on the male figure. The major chakras are shown as black ovals and the minor chakras as smaller grey circles. A reminder - the minor chakras are all bilateral (either side of the body's centre line), unless you include the two out of body chakras and the elusive spleen chakra mentioned earlier. There is sometimes little external indication that a chakra requires balancing, so it is "best practice" to balance them all anyway but with a little more emphasis on any you have stimulated and any you suspect intuitively may require attention. However, we must be realistic. Time or other circumstances may prevent a full treatment, especially if you are working in conjunction with another therapy. In that case, you can balance the ones we have stimulated and also, if possible the navel and heart chakras. As we will later see, the navel chakra is associated with the psychological quality of empowerment, much needed to aid recovery from illness, anxiety or depression. The heart chakra, in addition to its well known association with love, is often thought of as a bridge between the higher and lower chakras. The technique used is somewhat similar to acupressure, though the location is often different. If you have training in a meridian based therapy, you will need to put to one side your habit of precise acupoint location. The location of a minor chakra may not be on a meridian, though it probably will be. Which finger we choose to use is largely a matter of convenience, the position of the therapist and personal preference. Most practitioners would, I suspect favour the middle finger most of the time. The pad of the finger, rather than the fingertip should be used. On the more accessible chakras, such as the heart, navel and sacral (four, three and two), the palm of the hand can be used to great effect. Remember, the palm houses a powerful minor chakra.

Figure 4 – Chakra balancing, first stage.

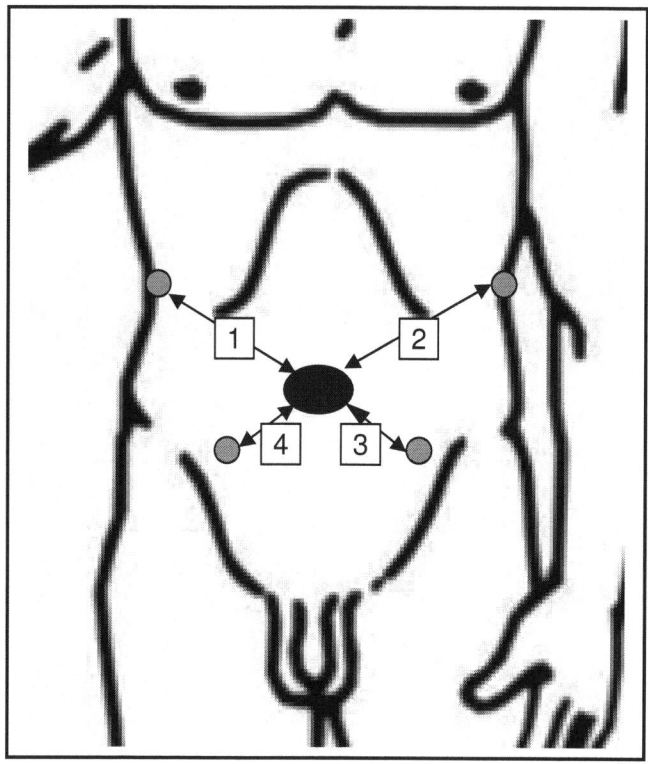

Figure 5 – Chakra balancing, second stage.

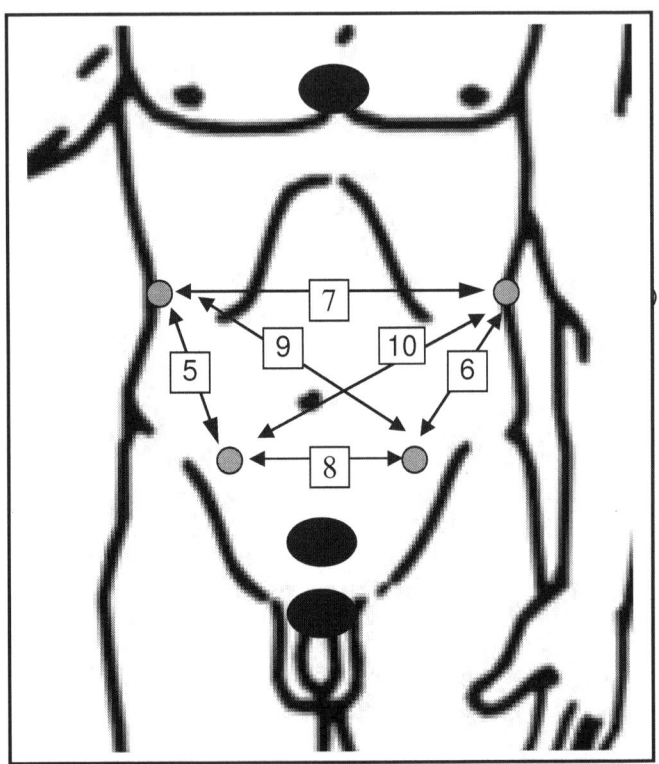

We will use the navel chakra *(manipura)* as an example. Take a good look at figures 4 and 5. The numbers do *not* relate to the chakras themselves but to the steps in our procedure. The intercostal chakras indicated by the double arrow 7 (figure 5) are situated on the side of the body towards the lower end of the ribcage. With the arms straight, alongside the body, they line up roughly with the elbow crease. We do not use the elbow chakra in this exercise.

If in doubt, we can easily locate it using the dowsing technique discussed in the previous chapter. Ask your client to lie on their side with the upper arm over the side of the head, so the side of the ribcage is exposed. We can then use the pendulum as we did in chapter 6. Incidentally, the left intercostal chakra will swing in the opposite direction to the right, a principle that applies to all the bilateral (two sided) minor chakras. Contrary motion can confirm that we have got things right and that we are not unconsciously cheating by moving the hand.

The lower pair, which I call the pelvic chakras, is situated near the end of the groin crease but *inside* the crease by about two fingers width.

CHAKRA BALANCING, FIRST STAGE

- Map the relevant chakras first and keep a mental note of their location. You can use the dowsing technique or finger sensation and intuition if you feel you are sensitive enough.
- Place either palm on the navel chakra with very light pressure.
- Place the pad of one finger on the right intercostal chakra as per "1" in figure 4 and hold for about 30 seconds. You should feel a faint sensation under the finger and palm not unlike the "fizzing" we experienced in our preliminary exercise in chapter 2, only weaker.
- When the sensation between the two feels similar, we are ready to move on to the next stage marked "2" in the illustration.
- Work your way round to "4", then the palm can be taken off the navel chakra.
- The order of 1-4 can be varied for convenience if necessary.

CHAKRA BALANCING, SECOND STAGE

- Stage 2 (figure 5) should be done with a single finger of each hand. It has been placed on a second diagram with the major chakra deleted for the sake of clarity.
- Positions 7 and 8 are bilateral balances. 5 and 6 are unilateral and 9 and 10 diagonal. The diagonals are perhaps the most important, so should be left to the end. A little more time should be spent on them.
- For good measure, we can balance a major chakra with its neighbours, using a palm or fingertip – *provided* its neighbours are in good working order, of course. In the case of our example, we would put a palm or finger on the navel chakra and one on the heart chakra, followed by one on the navel and one on the sacral chakra.

So far, so good. We can use the same technique to balance any of the major chakras, except root (one) and crown (seven). Here we run into difficulties. In the case of seven, it is simply the geographical fact that it has no neighbouring minor chakras. In the case of one, we have two associated chakras but a major problem with cultural taboos about intimate contact.

Let's do the easy stuff first. Behind and below the crown lies a point of considerable significance, which is not a chakra. In yoga we call it bindu. It can be found easily and precisely on your own body.

- Place the middle fingertip of either hand on the back of your neck, between those two thick tendons that connect the trapezius muscles (upper back) to the occiput (back of the skull).
- Slowly move the finger up the back of the head. It will pass over a roundish ridge and onto a flattish part of the back of the skull.
- Keep going until you find a very small indentation, just below the crown. At this stage, you may have to search about a bit, as you may have gone "off centre".
- The little indentation, smaller than a grain of rice, is the external manifestation of bindu.

Now that we have found bindu on ourselves, it is easy enough to find it on our client. Incidentally, the technique of "finding it on yourself first" is an excellent way of learning anatomy, if you are a bit hazy in that department. Some of us do not enjoy a close relationship with our own bodies! Back to our subject. We treat bindu and brow chakra (six) as minor chakras and balance using the same technique we used for the heart chakra above. We place a finger or palm on the crown and a finger pad on bindu and hold until balanced. We then do the same, using the brow chakra. This might be easier with the client sitting upright for ease of access. Alternatively, ask the client to turn their head away from you. We can balance the crown chakra the other way round if that suits our personal style a bit better i.e. brow first, bindu second.

Now for the difficult stuff. Most cultures have deep seated taboos about intimate contact between people who are not in a sexual relationship. Sadly, that taboo occasionally extends to those *inside* such a relationship as well. We may not agree with these taboos but we cannot ignore them. To do so is a recipe for trouble. We have to bear in mind our own professional, cultural and emotional boundaries, as well as our client's boundaries. We are not gynaecologists or urologists. Gender has little to do with it - it is a matter of cultural sensitivity. I personally would not even ask a client if I might place a finger on their perineum and would always ask before placing a hand on the anterior (frontal) aspect of the sacral chakra.

Fortunately, there are ways round the problem. Take a look at figure 3 again. At the top of the legs are two pairs of minor chakras joined by double headed arrows. In my opinion, these are both external manifestations of one pair of minor chakras situated near the hip joint, which is situated deep inside the upper leg, where it joins the pelvis through a ball and socket arrangement. Therefore, we do not need to use the medial (central) "face", which is close to the genitals. We can use the lateral (side) "face" instead. With the arms fairly straight, down the sides of the body, this lateral aspect is found near the wrists. It is situated at or near the top of the femur (thighbone), which can easily be found by palpation along the outer thigh. We can also find it with our now familiar dowsing technique. That just leaves us with the perineal problem. Ask your client to place *their* middle finger on the perineum. Take hold of the free hand with your hand (as if shaking hands) and place a finger of your free hand on the appropriate minor chakra. We now have a continuous energy loop from major chakra to relevant minor chakra. It's a long loop, so you need to spend longer on it. There are no relevant minor chakras below root chakra, so balancing is rather simpler. We balance as above, then balance the two minor chakras bilaterally i.e. one finger on each.

As the treatment progresses, your client may experience an emotional release. This may manifest itself as a simple sigh or the client may become tearful or (very occasionally) angry. This is absolutely nothing to worry about for either of you. Far from being a problem, it means that the treatment is starting to work. Remember - chakras are not just physical centres, they are psychophysical centres. Ask the client how they *feel*. Console them if necessary. Reassure them that such emotional venting is perfectly natural and sometimes we have to feel worse before we feel better.

We must now turn our attention towards the minor chakras situated in the limbs. A reminder – prana is routed to the legs via the sacral and root chakras and the arms via the throat and heart chakras. It follows that the limb chakras are very useful when balancing and treating these major chakras and any condition that is geographically near them. The same applies in reverse, of course. For example, if our client has a painful knee, we can utilise the sacral chakra.

The procedure for limbs is simplicity itself. We place one palm or finger on the sacral or heart chakra and a finger on the crease of the knee or elbow. We then repeat the process with the foot or hand. We can also use the reflex points on the feet but more about that in the next chapter.

8. REFLEX POINTS

Most people have heard of reflexology, also known as zone therapy. It is a popular complementary therapy. Many readers will have had personal experience as a client or even be trained as a therapist. For those who have not had the pleasure of a reflexology session, a very brief and approximate description is in order. I do not claim to be a trained reflexologist. Styles vary but the therapist will probably start by massaging both feet thoroughly, noting any tender, rough or "lumpy" parts. Each sole is a "map" of zones, which correspond to various parts of the body. Having massaged the feet, the therapist will then pay special attention to the parts that are tender or correspond with the organic symptoms presented by the client. Thus, if the client complains of a lung condition, such as emphysema, special attention will be paid to the zone on the ball of the foot just back from the middle three toes. Techniques vary but usually include further localised "micro massage" and finger pressure of varying intensity.

In chakra therapy, we do not use the zones (though there is considerable potential for an imaginative hybrid therapy) but rather a series of reflex points on the foot, which each relate to a specific major chakra. They can be thought of as echoes or reflections of the corresponding chakra. They are shown on figure 6. There are also reflex points on the hand, which are generally considered to be less effective but are very useful in cases where the foot is not within easy reach of the associated chakra. They are shown on figure 7. The medial side of the foot, in effect represents the spine and each point is associated with both the posterior (rear) and anterior (frontal) aspect of the corresponding chakra, so we can work on the front or back of the body. We must also remember the presence of the secondary foot chakra in the middle of the sole. We can use these reflex points to stimulate or balance any major chakra.

- Massage both feet gently. If your client is ticklish, this can be omitted. A moderate amount of oil can be used but it should be 100% natural, such as olive or grapeseed oil.
- Place a finger pad or palm on the relevant major chakra and a finger on the associated reflex point shown in figures 6 and 7. For the sake of clarity, I have kept to numbers, rather than names.
- Hold for at least 30 seconds, until sensation and intuition indicate a balance.
- Do the same with the same point on the other foot or hand.
- Take the finger or hand off the chakra and gently press *left and right* reflex points, holding for about 30 seconds.
- We have now completed the reflex balancing and stimulation of the chakra.
- We can now move on to any other chakra that requires treatment or round up the session by remapping the principal chakras to confirm that all is in order.

The above techniques may not be necessary but they are a useful addition to the clinical toolkit in cases where normal stimulation or balancing fail to deliver. If the client is severely debilitated and anxious, it is a gentle way to ease them into full chakra work.

Figure 6 – Approximate locations of the principal chakra reflex points on the feet. The grey circles indicate the minor foot chakras.

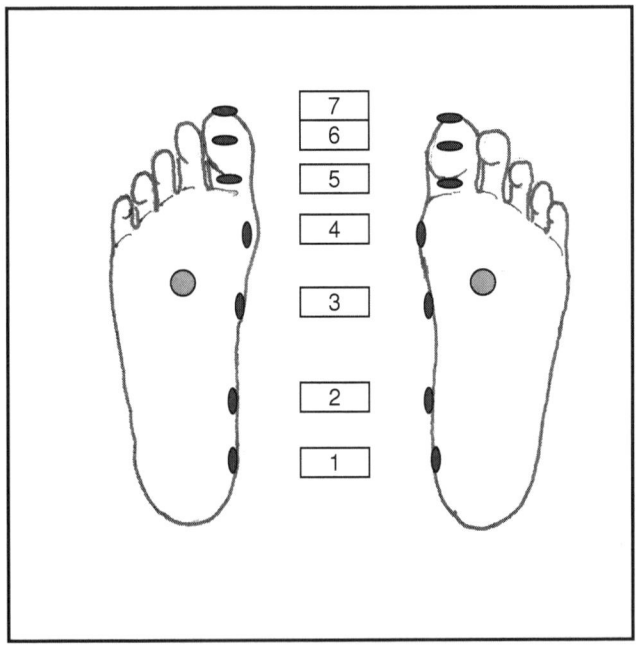

Figure 7 – Approximate locations of the principal chakra reflex points on the hands. The grey circles indicate the minor hand chakras.

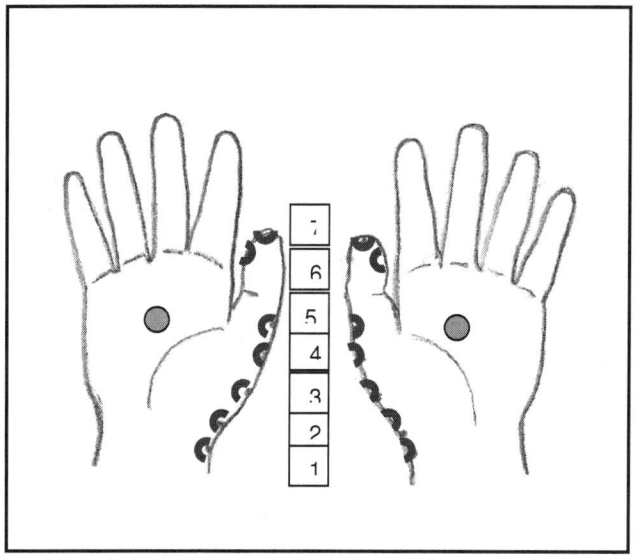

An important final point – there is no way of *objectively* confirming these reflex point locations. Opinions vary and we should consider them as our "best shot", rather than set in concrete.

9. WORKING ON THE BACK

In his book "Healing with the Chakra Energy System", John Cross asserts that problems with the musculo-skeletal system tend to respond better when treated with the posterior (rear) aspect of the chakras i.e. with the client lying prone and organic and emotional complaints tend to respond better when treated with the anterior (frontal) aspect i.e. with the client lying supine. I have no reason to doubt this self-evident assertion. The only problem we have is the lack of convenient landmarks on the back to guide us - unless our client is undressed and we have a thorough knowledge of the anatomy of the spinal column. I will assume that neither is the case. Further, we must once again remember that positions are not absolute and that my positions may be at variance with those given in other books. Map carefully, is the answer to any doubts.

As discussed earlier, chakras one and seven have only one manifestation (though we can find them easily with the client supine or prone), so they need not concern us, except to consider once again the question of cultural taboos on intimate contact. When using chakra two, a finger or hand on the sacrum is rather less threatening than a finger or hand on the pubis. Further, if you need to ask the client to remove any clothing, the prone position tends to overcome the embarrassment factor for both client and therapist.

The sacrum is a heart-shaped, knobbly bone at the base of the spine, above the gluteal cleft. It has major structural importance and if your knowledge of anatomy is shaky, you should most definitely locate it on yourself and preferably on a friend or partner as well. Its outline is usually apparent if the client is unclothed and easy to locate by touch through clothing. I mention this as I am aware that some "hands off" therapies require minimal knowledge of anatomy. The second chakra is usually located near the lower end of the sacrum, hence the designation "sacral". I must emphasise again at this point the posterior manifestation of a chakra is not necessarily on a vertical axis from the anterior (frontal) aspect. The axis may tilt a little, though usually the tilt is small, so the anterior presentation is a reasonably good guide. If we have any doubts about locating chakra three (navel), we can use the natural downward curve of the lumbar spine, when the client is prone. It can be found somewhere near the lowest point of the curve and near the waistband. Again, there are variations, so this signpost must be considered approximate. We can use the same technique for chakra four (heart), which is usually found at or near the upper point of the natural outer curve of the thoracic vertebrae. Chakra five (throat) is the one most likely to sit on a tilted axis. It is likely to be higher up the spine that it is on its anterior aspect. If your client has their face downwards, through a face hole in the treatment couch, the brow chakra is also easy to find, near the top of the rounded curve of the back of the skull. We should always map the chakras in the same way that we do when the client is supine. That will clear up any doubts about locations and once again tell us which require treatment or special emphasis.

Fortunately, most of the minor chakras I have been able to identify are still easily accessed when the client is prone, with the exception of the shoulder chakras. Attempts to find a posterior manifestation have been inconclusive, so my advice is to try to locate with the pendulum and if you get no result, ask your client to lift their shoulder a little, so you can access the frontal aspect with a finger. The actual technique for balancing and stimulating is identical to that used on a supine client.

10. TREATING SPECIFIC DISORDERS

In chakra therapy (as in many complementary therapies) the emphasis is on treating the whole person, so that prana levels are raised, the chakras harmonised and disease and injury symptoms are alleviated as soon as possible. It is an aid to natural recovery, not an antidote to symptoms. Therefore, most of the treatment is the same, regardless off the medical diagnosis. Only the emphasis varies. Below is a very approximate procedure, which will naturally vary from client to client and therapist to therapist. A degree of creative thought is needed.

BACKGROUND

- Ask the client if they have had a formal medical diagnosis. If they haven't, they should have one, even if they have little confidence in it. However, you should not refuse to treat the client until they have seen a doctor, simply advise them of the importance of a proper diagnosis.
- Pain, especially severe pain, should *always* be clinically investigated.
- Make notes about the diagnosis and presenting symptoms.
- Find the actual location of the problem. If necessary, ask the client to place a finger on the affected place.
- Explain briefly what you are about to do if it is a new client, unfamiliar with the treatment. An explanatory handout sheet or leaflet is a good idea.
- If the problem is musculo-skeletal, ask the client to lie prone. If it is organic or psychological/emotional, ask them to lie supine.

PRACTICE

- Ask the client to deepen their breath a little, without forcing.
- Map all the major chakras and stimulate any that are "down" and correct any that are reversed.
- Balance all the major chakras.
- Rebalance the major chakra nearest the problem area or organ.
- Rebalance any other major chakra that is associated with the problem organ, emotion or body part. These associations are itemised in the next chapter.
- If the problem is musculoskeletal, do not put any pressure (even light pressure) directly on the lesion site. You can, however, place a "healing hand" directly over the lesion site, without touching it. Use a neighbouring chakra if the lesion coincides with the position of a chakra. Gently massage *around* the lesion site, before balancing.
- Map the major chakras again to make sure they are still in balance.
- Keep a record of everything you have done, including any advice given.

We must *always* remember that we are dealing with *one unified organism,* rather than separate parts of the organism. The flip side of that coin is of course, that most illnesses are disorders of the whole organism, even if they manifest in a localised condition. Each chakra is connected to all the others but there is also a hierarchy of links. Firstly come the neighbours, secondly the links shown in figure 8 (which are somewhat speculative, so need not be adhered to rigidly) and thirdly, the rest. Excluding the limbs, the minor chakras are linked to both their neighbouring major chakras and to their neighbouring minor chakras as discussed in Chapter 7. Each individual minor chakra is also linked powerfully to its diagonally neighbouring minor chakra - e.g. the left shoulder is linked to the right ear and the right intercostal, and so on. Minor chakras on the limbs are obviously linked to their neighbours but also to the *opposite, other* limb chakra, so the right foot is linked to the left hand, the right knee to the left elbow and the right elbow to the left hip and vice versa.

Figure 8 – Major chakra links.

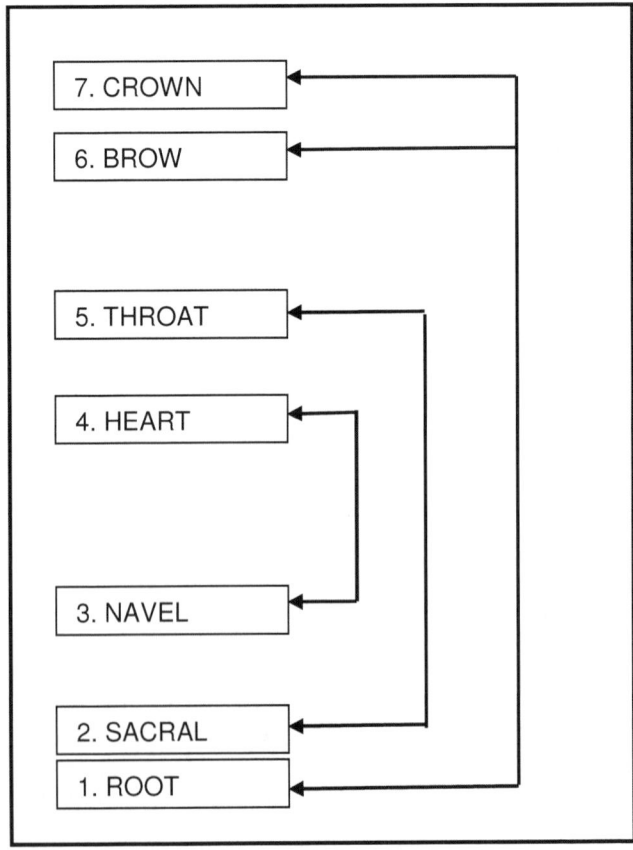

11. CONNECTIONS

We have seen in Chapter 10 that chakras have a hierarchy of links to each other. They also clearly have links to specific organs and systems in the body and also to emotional and psychological states. It is for very good reason that they are sometimes called "psycho-physical centres". Some of these links must be by their very nature speculative but much is self evident. A chakra will, for example influence anything that is anatomically near it. So sexuality is governed, by common consensus by the sacral chakra but common sense indicates that the root chakra, a close neighbour, must also have an effect. So both chakras should be treated in depth when sexual or reproductive symptoms are presented. The close proximity of the brow and crown chakras should also be born in mind. The chart below should be considered as a rough but useful guide, rather than the final word. Emotional and psychological links *are shown in italics.* By way of a reminder, it also shows (by means of double headed arrows) the links between the chakras discussed in the previous chapter.

7. CROWN. Brain, eyes. *Spiritual concerns. Sense of detachment. Higher consciousness.*

1. ROOT. Spinal column, urinary system, legs, feet, lower bowel. *Grounding, Sense of belonging. Sense of identity. Attachment and security.*

6. BROW. Brain, nervous system, ears, nose, eyes. Left/right balance. *Sleep and waking cycle. Perception, Intuition. Intellect. Wisdom.*

5. THROAT. Bronchial tubes, lungs, vocal chords, alimentary tract, throat, skin. Neck and arms. *Speech and communication.*

2. SACRAL. Reproductive system, fluid balance, lymphatics. Pelvis, legs, buttocks and genitals. *Sex and sexuality. Pleasure, joy and humour.*

4. HEART. Cardiovascular system, arms, vagus nerve, lymphatics. *Unconditional and universal love. Compassion. Bridge between the "higher" and "lower" self. Gratification. Gratitude.*

3. NAVEL. Stomach, liver, spleen, pancreas, duodenum, gallbladder. *Empowerment. Confidence. Ability to get things done. Self esteem.*

12. SELF THERAPY – A BACKGROUND

I am aware of the fact that this is not a "how to" book about yoga. There are enough of those on the market anyway – too many, some might argue. However, my sincere opinion is that any therapy that does not offer the client "something to take home" in the form of exercise, mental discipline or life style/diet changes is severely diminished. Further, we must also bear in mind the needs of the therapist, who needs to maintain good vitality in order to do the job properly. If the therapist fails to look after himself, burnout and breakdown are likely. A degree of self-help is therefore essential for both parties. It is the duty of the therapist to gently encourage the client on the self-help journey, even if he chooses to ignore advice. Paper handouts, of the sort handed out by colleges are a very useful addition to the toolkit. If you lack the computer skills or hardware, ask a computer owning friend to help you. Better still, enrol on a College course and update your skills. I take an inordinate amount of pride in my handouts but they don't have to be literary masterpieces. Sadly, the sick (and even the not so sick) sometimes slide into a victim psychology, where they feel helpless and expect all the curative input to come from the therapist. This mindset can be a major obstacle to recovery. The client needs to be reassured that they are not a victim of anything; they are suffering from something *at this moment in time.* There may not be any miracle cures but there is a lot that can be done to alleviate most conditions substantially.

I am reminded of a story told to me by a yoga colleague who specialised in teaching the sick and disabled. A man showed up who was suffering from Multiple Sclerosis, and was understandably angry at having to give up his business because of his poor health. "I want to know what you're going to do help me", he asked, somewhat abruptly. "Absolutely nothing", replied my colleague. The man went almost purple with rage. "But – I'm going to show you what you can do for yourself". He was immediately mollified. Apart from a concluding summary, the rest of this book is mostly (though not entirely) devoted to self-help for the chakras. You can use it for yourself – or you can teach it to your clients. You can ignore some of it but please don't ignore all of it!

Almost any form of self therapy or exercise is beneficial and the chapters that follow are most definitely not an attempt to be comprehensive. I have made no attempt to include related disciplines, such as qigong, tai chi and Pilates – simply because there are many excellent books and teachers around who could do a much better job in areas where my own knowledge is limited. If you are a therapist and one or more of these disciplines is "your thing", then some (but definitely not all) of what follows may be redundant to you personally but almost certainly won't be for your client. Further, the yoga content in the self-therapy that follows is not just the tip of the iceberg; it is the tip of the tip of the iceberg. Yoga is a very big subject. There is absolutely no substitute for a course with a good teacher, ongoing tuition and a good reference book (I have a whole shelf of them) to assist with home practice. However, you or your client may well be resistant to the idea, so the following is a helpful sampler to assist, rather than a serious technical manual for the would-be yogi. Some of what follows is not really part of the yoga tradition, though where we draw the line is a matter of some debate. Yoga has always had fuzzy boundaries. Another point – yoga teachers usually have strong opinions on what constitutes good, effective practice and most have areas of special interest. I certainly have. I have therefore made no attempt to be objective is this little survey. It is based largely on personal experience, practicality and preference – as all good yoga should be.

13. THE USE OF SOUND

Sound has been used to assist healing since ancient times. It is sometimes used in conjunction with dance, singing or simple, rhythmic handclapping. It is sometimes devotional and sometimes abstract. Style and personal preference play a big part. If you are not religious, don't be put off. You don't *have* to use anything devotional – there are plenty of alternatives. At the other end of the faith spectrum, if you have a strongly focussed religious ideology, many of the sounds and chants are abstract or spiritual in a generalised way. Incidentally, chanting is *not* specifically a Hindu or Buddhist practice. There are many Christian, Jewish and Islamic chants.

MANTRA – A mantra is a chant (usually but not always brief), which is repeated over and over until a change of consciousness is induced. Many (but by no means all) mantras are chanted in Sanskrit or Pali (a derivative of Sanskrit believed to be the mother tongue of the Buddha). I have to admit that I started out in yoga as a convinced mantra sceptic. As a teacher with a secular approach, I could find neither use nor reason for it, until I experienced an amazing group aum chant at a training day. I was blown away. I am now convinced of the value of the aum chant, even if I remain doubtful about some of the others. It sets up a vibration through the chakras that has to be experienced to be appreciated.

The symbol above is the visual representation of AUM. It is not Sanskrit but probably a very ancient pre-Sanskrit pictogram. Its origins are obscure. AUM or OM represents the totality and intangible unity of the universe and all that is in it, known and unknown – "everything that was, everything that is, everything that will be".

It is the spiritual manifestation of a philosophical school known in India as Vedanta ("end of the Vedas"). In the West, this concept of the unity of all things is known as Monism. Aum is also thought of as the primordial sound of the universe. In my view, it should not therefore be thought of as devotional but abstract. The AUM chant is appropriate for yogins of all beliefs and none. When spoken or chanted it is usually pronounced AUM and when written or thought about silently OM. Mantras generally can be visualised, rather than sounded aloud or even whispered, though both these methods are, in my view pale imitations of the real thing. However, if you have serious hang-ups about vocalising, even in private, it may well be worth experimenting with these methods.

Chanting is one of mankind's oldest cultural expressions. We were chanting long before we were singing. It awakes within us an almost primal feeling that is impossible to describe in words. The fact that it now often sounds "weird" or "a bit odd" is a sad reflection on how we have lost touch with our true selves. Be brave and "Don't knock it 'til you've tried it" is the best advice I can give.

- When chanted, AUM is actually 4 sounds rolled into one. The sounds should merge almost imperceptibly. The A and U are long, the M is a humming sound and the tongue is lifted to the roof of the mouth in the second part of the M to produce a more nasal sound. So the whole sounds a bit like "AAAAAUUUUUMMMMMMMnMnMnMnMnMn.." Naturally, this is only an approximation. Like all yoga, it has to be experienced rather than read about.

- When chanting, great emphasis should be placed on good posture and correct breathing (the two are interdependent). Any comfortable seated position is fine provided the spine is upright but relaxed. Nothing at all should inhibit the breath. Tight clothing, slumped posture and drooping head are all "no go". Close the eyes. Take a really big deep breath in, relax the throat, and then go for it! Continue until the lungs are nearly empty. Then take another deep breath and repeat as many times as desired. Three is a popular number for group chanting but the more the better.

- In a group AUM chant, no attempt should be made to keep together. The overlapping entries, with the sound almost floating in the air, are all part of the experience and effect. In an effective group chant, the whole room will seem to vibrate.

- Chanting is *not* the same as singing. Correct intonation and beauty of tone are completely unimportant. Good breathing, confidence and a sincere delivery count for much more. It is *not* performance art. If your voice sounds like an overworked angle grinder, it doesn't really matter!

BIJA MANTRAS (bija = "seed") are single syllable sounds used in conjunction with aum to stimulate specific major chakras in turn. They are chanted in the same way, at least three times each. Below is a chart of the bija mantras, which tend to vary a little according to source. My own experience is that aum does nicely for all of them but bija mantras can be used in chakra meditation. More on that later. The bija can be sounded silently to oneself but in my experience this is far less effective, though once again, useful for those who are inhibited about vocalising. The same chanting technique is used that we use for AUM, so LAM is sounded "LLLAAAAAMMMMnMnMn" and so on.

NUMBER	NAME	LOCATION	BIJA MANTRA
7	SAHASRARA	CROWN	AUM
6	AJNA	BROW	AUM
5	VISHUDDHI	THROAT	HAM
4	ANAHATA	HEART	YAM
3	MANIPOORA	NAVEL	RAM
2	SWADHISTANA	SACRUM	VAM
1	MULADARA	PERINEUM	LAM

Mantra is a big subject. There's a lot more to it than this "toe in the water" sketch, which suffices as a simple therapeutic tool. If you have a serious personal interest, it is well worth investing in one of many excellent books and CDs around and attend a workshop for some live tuition. A mantra master is something of a specialist – he/she will probably know hundreds of different mantra but possibly less well informed about other, more physical aspects of yoga. If you're a yoga purist, all of the above is within the yoga tradition. *Mantra yoga is simply another form of yoga and just as valid as any other, though less widely practiced.*

ABSTRACT SOUNDS are also highly effective if you are culturally uncomfortable with traditional mantra. Below is a table of easy to make sounds, using a similar technique to the bija mantras. My view, based on personal experience only, is that they are rather more effective than the bija mantras. Again, good breathing, posture and uninhibited sounding are of paramount importance.

NUMBER	LOCATION	SOUND
7	CROWN	Ngngng as in "bring"
6	BROW	Mmm or nnn
5	THROAT	Ee as in "see"
4	HEART	Ay as in "play"
3	NAVEL	Ah as in "father"
2	SACRUM	Oo as in "boo"
1	ROOT	Oh as in "boat"

Attempts have been made to associate notes of the musical scale with the chakras, so C is associated with the root, D with the sacral and so on. In my view, these attempts are misguided and unconvincing, though I remain open to persuasion to the contrary. When we talk of "C", which octave are we in? A low bass C will have a quite different effect from a high treble C. Further, concert pitch is a relatively modern concept. The present "A440" ("middle A" = 440 cycles per second) standard was only adopted as recently as 1939 as the result of an international conference. The actual division of the octave into its separate notes is also problematical. Today, the twelve notes (including semitones) are the result of a division into exactly equal divisions, hence the term "equal temperament tuning". This method (then a very modern idea) was strongly advocated by J.S.Bach, who composed his celebrated 48 preludes and fugues for just such a tuning system. It was not always so. "Mean temperament tuning" (a more natural but less flexible method) and occasionally, one or two other more eccentric tuning systems were in use prior to that time.

The association of musical notes with the chakras is both cautionary and instructive. It is a psychologically interesting example of how we can get carried away by coincidence and the power of numbers, especially if such numbers are deemed auspicious. Seven (major) chakras, seven notes, 7=7 so there must be a link! Not necessarily so, of course. However, it is fair to say that the lower the pitch of the sound, the lower the effect on the physical body, so pitch your "oh" as low as you can comfortably manage.

14. POSTURES AND OTHER PRACTICES

I firmly believe that the body is the gateway to the soul. The body is tangible, the mind is intangible. My personal experience and training confirms this self-evident truth. We can therefore often access the deeper layers of our mind (and its conflicts) through the body. There is nothing new or radical about this idea. It has been known about in India for at least 2000 years and in the West, the groundbreaking therapeutic work of Wilhelm Reich over eighty years ago on what he called character armour[1] demonstrated conclusively that the "bodymind" was not just a mystical Eastern construct, it was a tangible, verifiable reality. The purpose of the exercises in this chapter is therefore to loosen the armour (muscular tension, in everyday parlance) and allow prana to flow freely and energise the chakras.

It follows from the above that it is easy to become overly analytical, when selecting practices for individual chakras. For example, in the previous chapter I quoted traditional yoga wisdom that the aum chant stimulates the top two chakras. Common sense indicates, however that it must also stimulate the throat chakra, as that is where the sound originates. Personal experience acquired by regular practice tells me that it also stimulates the heart and navel chakras as well and I like to think that, directly or indirectly, it influences all the chakras, though not on a conscious level. Most of these practices likewise work on the whole body – it is only the emphasis that varies. Because of their close proximity, I have therefore considered the first two chakras (root and sacral) as being identical from an exercise standpoint. I have kept the top two (brow and crown) separate but there is likewise a degree of overlap. Rest assured that if you use the wrong exercise, it won't do you any harm! Not all of the exercises belong inside the yoga tradition, which has rather fuzzy boundaries anyway. Some I have devised myself, though I claim no credit for this – it is

---

[1] Reich, W. *Character Analysis.*

perfectly possible, indeed likely, that someone has been there before me. Others are bioenergetic type exercises. Bioenergetics[2] is a therapy and exercise system pioneered by Alexander Lowen, who was a pupil of Wilhelm Reich. It is well worth investigating if you are allergic to yoga.

With any form of exercise, consideration must be given to factors such as age, fitness and natural ability. Once again, live tuition with an experienced teacher is preferable, though all these practices have been carefully selected so that they are safe for all except the most unfit and debilitated. The golden rule is to move *slowly,* and then if anything starts to hurt, you can stop or ease up before any damage is done. Any posture where the head is below the heart should be avoided if you have hypertension (high blood pressure) or serious eye or ear problems.

* *For clarity and ease of execution, I have spaced most of these practices out one per page and used a larger font size.*

CHAKRAS one & two (root and sacral).

(A) Star posture (Bhadrasana). Figure 9

1. Sit on the floor (or try a yoga block if you have one), with the knees bent and the soles of the feet pressed together. There should be a gap between heels and crotch.

2. Clasp the hands together and grip the feet firmly, pulling into the body as close as possible.

3. Breathe in, straighten up and relax the hips.

---

[2] Lowen, A. *The Way to Vibrant Health – A Manual of Bioenergetic Exercises.*

4. On the out breath, bend the elbows, passing them in front of the shins and downwards. When they have reached their limit, press them firmly onto the shins. You should be able to feel an "opening out" action within the hips.

5. Hold for about 20-30 seconds, breathing as normally as possible, increasing with practice to 40-60 seconds.

6. Breathe in and straighten up, releasing the feet.

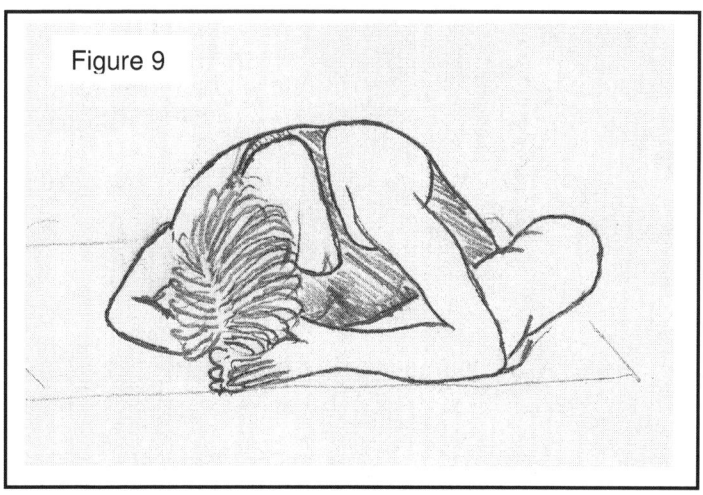

Figure 9

(B) Bridge Posture *(Dwi Pada Pittam).* Figure 10

1. Lie on the back with the knees bent and the feet about hip width apart. The heels should be fairly close the body, so the shins are vertical.

2. Take a deep breath in.

3. On the out breath, lift the buttocks off the floor and push the hips up into a back arch.

4. Hold for 20-30 seconds breathing normally through the nose. This can be increased to 40-60 seconds with practice.

5. On the out breath, lower slowly down, until the whole of the back is flattened into the floor.

6. Draw the knees up towards the chest and clasp them.

7. On the out breath, hug the knees firmly into the chest, holding for a few seconds.

8. Repeat step 7 two more times.

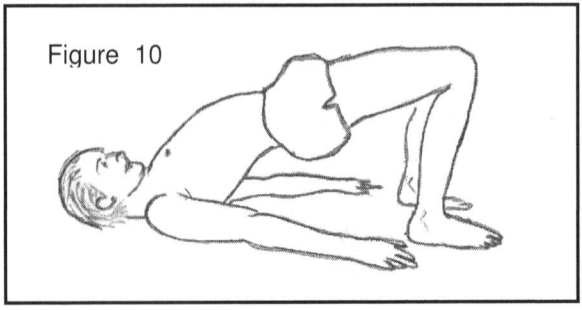

Figure 10

(C) Pelvic Breath or Pelvic Tilt.

In this exercise, the buttocks should not lift off the floor. All the conscious movement is in the lower back, which is where we should focus our attention.

1. Lie on the back with the knees bent and the feet about hip width apart. The heels should be fairly close to the body, so the shins are vertical.

2. Breathe out strongly.

3. As you breathe in again, hollow up the lower back, so there is room to slide a hand underneath.

4. As you breathe out, flatten the lower back into the floor, so the whole of the back is in contact with the floor.

5. Repeat another nine times or more if desired.

CHAKRA 3 (Navel).

(A) Supine Twist *(Jathara Parivritti).* Figure 11

1. Lie on the back with the knees bent, this time the feet and knees should be close together – pressing into one another. The arms should be out to the sides at shoulder level, palms downwards.

2. Take a deep breath in.

3. On the out breath, slowly roll the knees over to the right (don't worry if they don't go to the floor), then turn the head to the left, looking along the left arm. Keep breathing all the time.

4. Hold for 30-60 seconds.

5. On the out breath, slowly roll the knees and head back up to centre and pause for a few seconds.

6. Repeat the other way round.

If you find you have a "bad" and "good" side (a common problem), spend a little longer on the less mobile side.

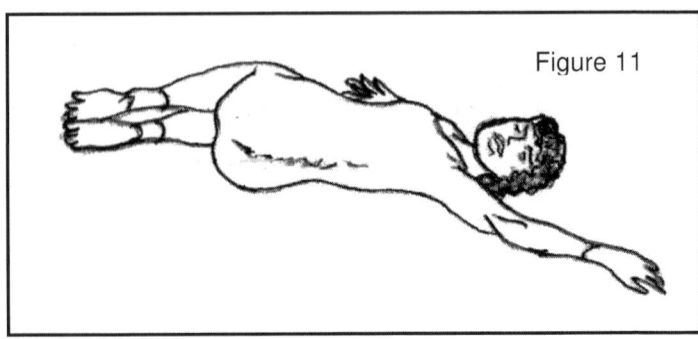

Figure 11

(B) Abdominal Retraction *(Uddiyana Bandha)*.
Figure 12

! Do not attempt this one if you have any abdominal problems !

1. Stand with the feet about shoulder width apart, feet turned out slightly.

2. Bend the knees and place the hands on the thighs, just back from the knees.

3. Breathe out very strongly and hold the breath out.

4. Pull the abdominal wall in and up, as if you are trying to suck the stomach into the ribcage.

5. Hold for about ten seconds.

6. Relax the abdomen, straighten up and allow the air back into the lungs slowly.

7. After fully mastering the retraction, it should be performed three times.

N.B. In the early stages, the retraction should only be held for about 5 seconds, gradually working up to 10 seconds with practice.

82

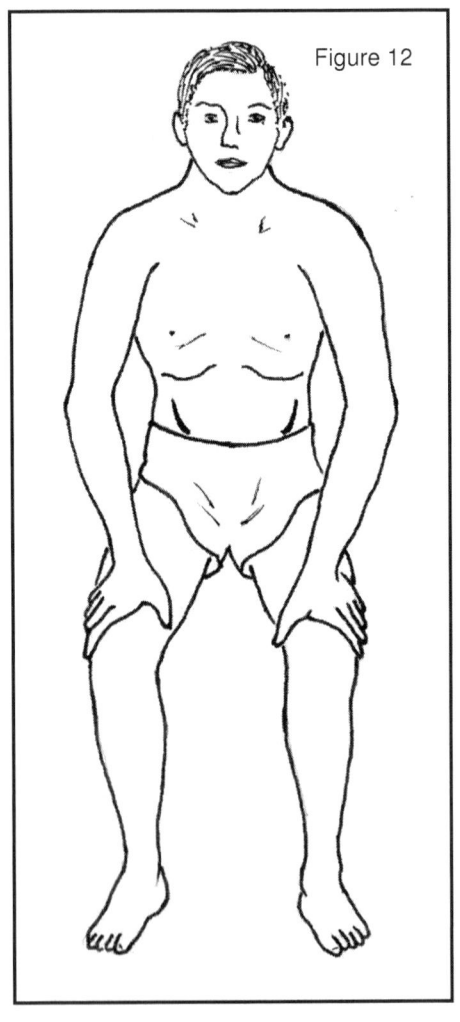

Figure 12

CHAKRA FOUR (Heart).

(A) Cobra *(Bhujangasana).* Figure 13

! Care should be taken with this posture if you have any history of lower back pain !

1. Lie prone (flat on the stomach) with the feet together, the head centred and the palms in line with the eyes, shoulder width apart and the fingers pointing forward.

2. Breathe in deeply.

3. On the out breath, *slowly* lift the head, then the chest, draw the elbows in and *nearly* straighten the arms, as in the illustration.

4. Keep the pelvis on the floor. If it lifts and you can't keep it down, bend the elbows a little more or even keep them on the floor. (See below).

5. Hold the posture for 20-30 seconds, breathing slowly and deeply.

6. Lower slowly down, turning the head to one side.

For a gentler version, leave the elbows on the floor, so the weight of the upper body is resting on the forearms. This is the sphinx posture.

For a more advanced version, straighten the arms completely and *carefully* tilt the head back to look upwards.

Almost any other back bend that opens out the chest is also effective.

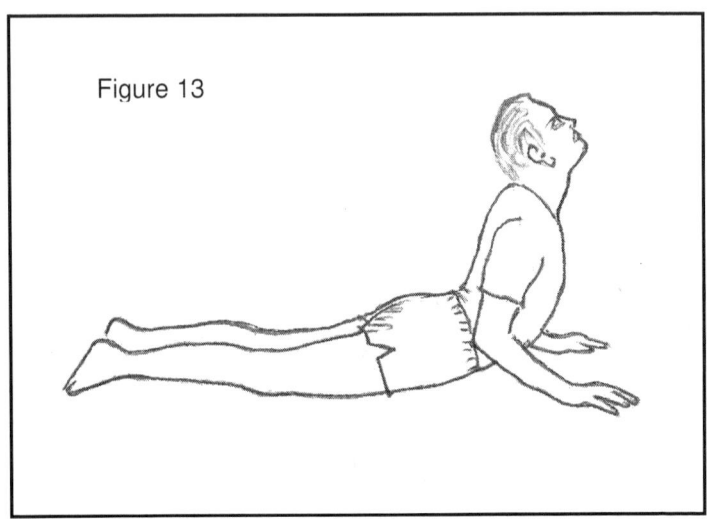

Figure 13

(B) Standing Back Bend. Figure 14

Alexander Lowen called this one "the bow" but that is used as the name of a quite different yoga posture, so I have given it my own name.

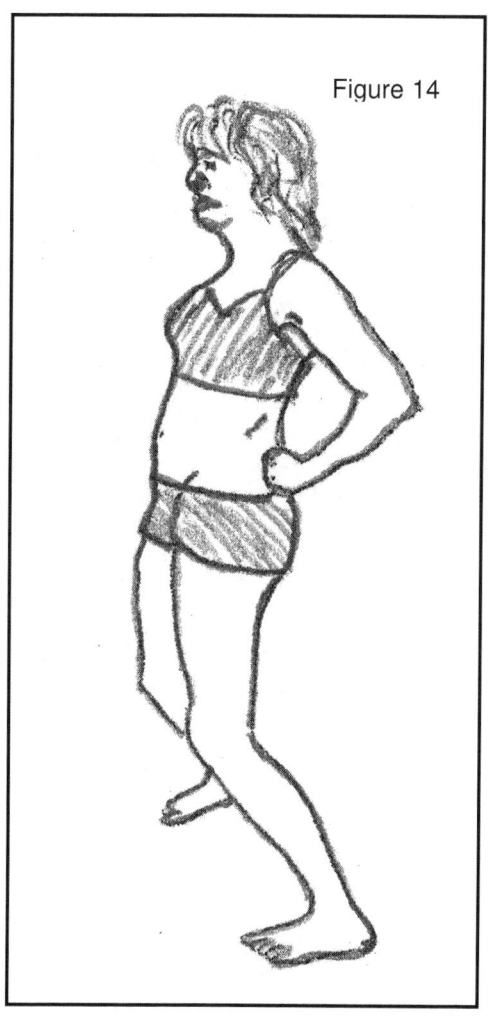

Figure 14

1. Stand with the feet about shoulder width apart and the knees relaxed.

2. Clench the fists and press them firmly into the lower back.

3. Bend the knees but don't allow the heels to lift.

4. Push the hips forward and draw the shoulders back.

5. Tilt the head back *gently.*

6. Keep breathing slowly and deeply all the time.

7. Hold for about 20 seconds, increasing with practice to 40-60 seconds.

8. *Slowly* straighten up the body and realign the head.

∗ The weight should be on the balls of the feet but the heels should not lift off the floor.

CHAKRA FIVE (Throat).

(A) Aum chant. See chapter 13.

(B) Tongue seal *(Kechari Mudra).*

1. Assume any comfortable seated position with the back upright but relaxed.

2. Curl the tongue up and over, so that the underside presses firmly into the roof of the mouth. The lips should be closed but the teeth a little apart.

3. Hold for 20-30 seconds, longer if possible.

4. Release the tongue.

(C) Lion *(Simhasana).* **Figure 15**

This one is very useful for dealing with problems of unexpressed anger.

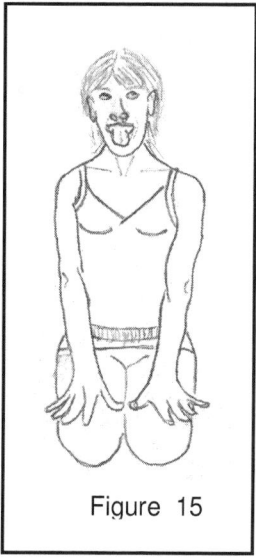

Figure 15

1. Sit on the heels with the thumbs pressed onto the knees and the fingers spread out wide.
2. Open the mouth and eyes very wide and tilt the head back.
3. Protrude the tongue as far as you can.
4. Breathe deeply through the mouth and nose.
5. If you feel brave enough, make a roaring sound by vocalising HAAAA!!! as loudly as possible. (Strictly optional!)

CHAKRA SIX (Brow).

(A) Aum chant. See chapter 13.

(B) Lion. See chakra 5.

(C) Eye rolling (1).

1. Sit on the heels as in the lion posture (or in a hard backed chair) but don't tilt the head back.

2. Turn the head slowly to the right, then to the left. Get into a natural, unforced rhythm. Keep breathing deeply all the time.

3. Without stopping, open the eyes wide (as if in fright) and as the head turns to the right, roll the eyes as far to the right as you can, to look over the right shoulder.

4. As you turn the head to the left, roll the eyes to the left as far as you can, to look over the left shoulder.

5. Keep up this slow rhythmic movement for 40-60 seconds, more if possible.

CHAKRA SEVEN (Crown).

(A) Hare Posture *(Pranamasana)*. Figure 16

1. Sit on the heels on the floor with the hands loosely gripping the ankles.

2. Breathe in.

3. On the out breath, lift the buttocks off the heels and tilt forward, lowering the crown onto the floor, without putting too much pressure on the head.

4. Hold for about 20-30 seconds, breathing normally.

5. Lower the buttocks down and tilt back up slowly.

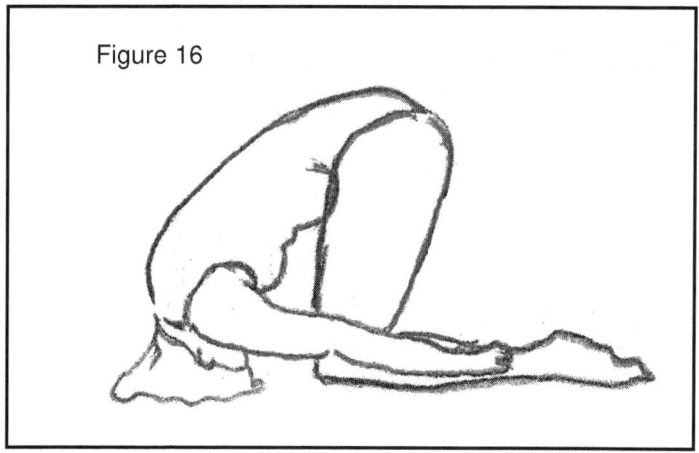

Figure 16

(B) Crown rub (1).

1. Place the palm of the right hand in contact with the top of the head.

2. Rub the head with a small circling movement of the hand, about 6 slow circles in each direction.

3. Do the same with the left hand.

(C) Crown rub (2).

1. Press the pad of the middle finger of either hand *firmly* onto the scalp at the top of the head.

2. Keeping a firm pressure, move the pad of the finger in a small circular movement, so that the scalp moves over the skull.

3. Repeat about ten times in each direction.

15. BREATHWORK

On the surface of things, the breath may seem to have little to do with chakras and their balance. In practice however, good breathing is crucial. We must always remember that prana is the fuel for the chakras. If prana is depleted, it is rather like trying to start a car engine with a flat battery. No amount of tinkering will get it going until the battery is recharged, hence the need to ask the client to consciously deepen their breathing while we are working with them and for the therapist to do the same.

This may not be enough, though. Most people have *unconscious* disordered breathing. This is often not diagnosed, unless there are clinical symptoms, such as asthma. The busy GP or hospital doctor rarely gets the chance to objectively observe a patient's normal breathing in the way that a trained yoga teacher does in a class situation. In the clinical situation, the apprehensive patient cannot possibly "be himself", so his normal, habitual breathing pattern is seldom observed. In my classes, I have observed breathing which is too fast, too shallow, jerky, gasping, "breath catching" and "breath amnesia", where the person breathes out and fails to breathe in again until an excessively long pause has elapsed. This latter phenomenon is rarely commented on or observed but in my opinion, is quite common.

The long-term effects of disordered breathing can be catastrophic. If we chronically under breathe *(hypoventilation)*, pranic levels are depressed (in addition to the more obvious oxygen deficit) and therefore the chakras are weakened or closed. Eventually, degenerative conditions such as cancer and arthritis are much more likely to manifest themselves. Over breathing *(hyperventilation)* will cause different problems. We are not now discussing the short-term effects of deliberate over breathing practiced in some breathwork exercises. We are discussing *chronic, habitual* over breathing.

The psychophysiology[1] of over breathing is too complex to explain in detail in this modest volume. Suffice it to say that it can actually cause the opposite of what we would expect, namely oxygen deficiency at cellular level. It can also cause alarming psychological problems such as panic attacks, though a continuous, nagging low-level anxiety state is a more common manifestation. This is caused by the expected pranic overcharge. The former is well known to medical science. A paper bag held over the face to raise carbon dioxide levels in the body is a well known first aid treatment for a disabling panic attack. The latter is more the preserve of those familiar with life energy. Both tend to trigger the well-known "fight or flight" response, which is actually a physiological response of the autonomic nervous system[2], which kicks into sympathetic[3] mode. This causes a fast pulse, high blood pressure and raised levels of adrenalin and noradrenalin amongst other things.

Now, all these things are highly desirable in a genuine "fight or flight" situation, such as being attacked by a wild animal but under normal, safe circumstances, the long term effects of such a chronic, "hyped up" state are disastrous. For example, most heart disease is caused by an overcharged energetic core, causing the heart to work too hard. Chronic hypertension (raised blood pressure) is the principal cause of most strokes and heart attacks.

---

[1] Physiology is the science of the physical body and its parts, so psychophysiology is the branch of physiology dealing with mental phenomena.

[2] The primitive or instinctive nervous system, mostly beyond our conscious control. It helps to regulate the functions of the internal organs, such as the heart, stomach, intestines etc.

[3] Sometimes called the orthosympathetic. It is the part of the autonomic system that, among other things, assists survival in stressful or dangerous situations.

Yogic breathing techniques are called *pranayama.* (*Prana* = breath/life force; *ayama* = extension/expansion). Many of them should only be attempted as part of a thorough training in hatha (physical) yoga with a good reference book[1] or (far better), an experienced teacher. The exercise described below, which is really "breath and movement", rather than pranayama can be attempted by anyone.

SUPINE PELVIC BREATH

1. Lie on the back with the knees bent, feet about hip width apart, palms facing downwards.
2. Breathe out strongly.
3. Breathe in slowly and as you do so, hollow the lower back and raise the arms "up and over", so the backs of the hands are on or near the floor behind the head.
4. Pause for one second.
5. As you breathe out, lower the arms down again and flatten the back into the floor.
6. Pause for one second.
7. Repeat another seven times.
8. The action and breath should be slow and smooth – completely unforced.
9. Over a period of about 4 weeks, gradually increase the number of breaths from 8 to 12.
10. Practice daily – more if possible.

---

[1] Try Asana Pranayama Mudra Bandha by Swami Satyananda Saraswati.

There are many other exercises like the one above. If you're allergic to yoga, it's worth investigating Qigong (chikung), a traditional Chinese discipline, which specialises in such practices. Qigong means "energy (prana) cultivation".

16. SWARA

Swara means "sound". More specifically, it is the sound of the air flowing through the individual nostrils. It is the difference between the sound of the two nostrils that tell us of the state of balance or imbalance between the two nadis, ida and pingala, which spiral round the central nadi, sushumna. (See chapter 4). Ida terminates at the left nostril and pingala at the right. Most of the time, one nostril dominates and the other is subordinate and the two sides change over roughly every 90-180 minutes, with a brief changeover period, when the two sides are in balance. At least, that is what is supposed to happen. However, sometimes the swara becomes "stuck", with one side dominating most or all of the time. When this happens, the person is more likely to suffer from illness[1]. Try this simple test on yourself. I used it to diagnose my own habitual left nostril breathing which I was able to correct, using the techniques described later.

- Breathe in.
- Close the right nostril with gentle finger pressure.
- Breathe out through the left nostril, carefully observing the sound and quality of the breath flowing through the nostril.
- Repeat the steps above, closing the left nostril and exhaling through the right nostril.
- One nostril will probably feel slightly closed and have a higher pitched, "dryer" sound. This is the subordinate nostril.
- Repeat the test at random times through the day. The balance between the two sides should alternate, as described above.

---

[1] Riga, Dr. I.N., quoted in *Kundalini Tantra* by Swami Satyananda Saraswati.

This slow, cyclical change from side to side has been associated with changes in the dominance of the two hemispheres of the brain. There is ample evidence that the cycle is essential for good mental and physical health. If you or your client has a sluggish swara, it is essential to take steps to remedy it. This is often easily done. The pranayama described below is very easy and suitable for those who do not have a yoga training.

SINGLE NOSTRIL BREATHING

- First, find your dominant nostril, as above.
- Breathe out fully and then close the dominant nostril with gentle finger pressure.
- Breathe in deeply and strongly through the subordinate nostril.
- Exhale slowly and softly, through the same nostril.
- Perform six breaths like this, followed by a full inhalation through both nostrils and a long, slow exhalation.
- Slowly increase the practice to twelve breaths and practice daily, more if possible.
- Any time of day is suitable but just before bedtime is ideal.
- Ideally, the exhalation should take twice as long as the inhalation, so if the inhalation takes four seconds, the exhalation should take eight. This may take a little time and practice to achieve. The exhalation should be smooth and soft, not jerky. Again, this takes practice to achieve.

If the subordinate nostril is blocked, it will be necessary to wait until it unblocks naturally or use a decongestant. Another practice is even easier. It is a type of unilateral chakra balancing. Remember that the brow chakra (6) is primarily responsible for the brain, eyes and nose.

UNILATERAL BROW CHAKRA BALANCING

- Find your dominant nostril again.
- Place one middle finger on the brow chakra. Apply very light pressure.
- Place the other middle finger on the secondary ear chakra (under the earlobe) on the *subordinate* side.
- Hold for at least a minute, breathing slowly and deeply.
- Practice daily, more often if possible.
- This one is easy to do with a client, provided the dominant nostril has been correctly identified. This requires work at home by the client, which they may be reluctant to do.

In my experience, self balancing is less effective than having someone else do it for you but it still works well enough to be worthwhile in this instance. In the therapy scenario, you can treat the client as above and teach them how to do the same thing themselves at home. There is a more sophisticated, if slightly fussy method that combines the two techniques in a highly effective personal practice.

COMBINATION TECHNIQUE

- Place whichever middle finger is convenient on the brow chakra.
- The thumb of the same hand is used to close the *dominant* nostril with gentle pressure.
- The middle finger of the other hand is placed on the *subordinate* ear chakra.
- Breathe through the *subordinate* nostril as per single nostril breathing but maintaining finger contact with the ear chakra all the time.
- Practice daily, more often if possible.
- Alternatively, we can employ the two techniques "back to back", so single nostril breathing, followed by unilateral brow chakra balancing.

Far more effective than any of the above, however is a traditional yoga *kriya* called *jala neti* or simply *neti*. It is a nasal irrigation technique, which is not nearly as unpleasant as it sounds. Indeed, once mastered, it is actually pleasantly refreshing. Despite all my reassurances, based on personal experience, my yoga students are rather reluctant to try it but I feel duty bound to discuss it from time to time. It requires an inexpensive piece of equipment called a neti pot. These are available from on-line yoga retailers. A neti pot looks rather like a small teapot, without a lid.

JALA NETI

- Dissolve half a teaspoonful of salt in half a pint of tepid water. (Sea salt is better but table salt will do). Make the solution stronger if you think you have an infection.
- Fill the neti pot.
- Over a basin, hold the pot in your left hand and tilt the head strongly to the right, so the bridge of the nose is horizontal. It helps to bend the knees and rest the right elbow on the right knee.
- Gently push the nozzle of the pot into your left nostril and tilt the pot, so that the solution trickles into the nostril and fills the nasal cavity behind the nose, then runs out of the right nostril. Allow the solution to flow for about 15 seconds.
- Remove the nozzle and straighten the neck. Allow the nose to drip into the basin for a few seconds, then repeat using the right nostril.
- Still over the basin, close the right nostril and blow strongly through the left.
- Repeat through the right nostril.
- Practice at least three times a week and daily if ear/nose/throat symptoms are troubling you.
- Any leftover solution makes a useful mouthwash and/or gargle.

Swara yoga is an almost forgotten art, long due for revival. The above techniques are mostly my own, rather than traditional yoga practice. *They do not take effect immediately. At least 5 minutes and usually much more are needed for any change to be manifested. More than one session may be required to begin with.* A degree of patience and perseverance is needed. For further in depth information for practicing yogis, I recommend an excellent book by the same name by Swami Muktibodhananda[1].

For centuries, Indian Ayurvedic[2] physicians have set great store on the principle of balanced breathing. The "nose job" is not a twentieth century Western invention. It was observed by medics from the British East India Company in the early days of British rule in India, though carried out for health, rather than cosmetic reasons.

---

[1] Muktibhodananda, Swami. *Swara Yoga – The Tantric Science of Brain Breathing*.
[2] *Ayurveda* is traditional Indian medicine, dating back to ancient Vedic times.

17. CHAKRA MEDITATIONS

If you (or your client) are "into" meditation, chakra meditations are powerful and effective, perhaps because the attention is turned inwards into the Self, rather than to an external object, real or imaginary. If you have never practiced meditation, a good "how to" book or, better still, a short course with "live" tuition is essential. Personal taste and availability will affect your choice of book, of course. One of my favourites is listed below.[1] Most meditation is practiced sitting and this is certainly true of chakra meditations. A comfortable seated posture is essential, to avoid distraction and/or slumping. If you cannot master one of the traditional yogic seated postures familiar from book covers and magazine articles (most people can't), sitting on a cushion or hard-backed chair is perfectly OK. *Never* try to force the legs into a cross-legged posture that they are not suited to – it is almost certain to cause injury. The spine should be upright but relaxed and the breath should flow easily and smoothly.

If you have little or no experience, learning to meditate requires patience and perseverance. Even experienced and gifted meditators sometimes have problems with the attention drifting and unwanted thoughts intruding. If this happens, we do not "beat ourselves up" with self accusation and judgement; we simply push the intruding thought gently to one side, put it on hold and pick up where we think we left off. We may have to do this several times, especially in the early stages.

---

[1] LeShan, L. *How to Meditate.*

- Assume a comfortable seated position. Make sure the hands are comfortable and not fidgety.
- Close the eyes. Observe the breathing passively, without trying to change it.
- Focus the attention onto the first chakra. Visualise it as a red vortex.
- Breathing naturally and continuing to visualise, count seven out breaths.
- Now shift the attention up to the second chakra. Visualise it as an orange vortex.
- Count seven out breaths.
- Work up the chakras using the colours red, orange, yellow, green blue and purple and finally, white for chakra seven (crown).
- Do the same working down from the crown to the root, using a lower number of out-breaths if you wish.
- Stop counting and just observe the breath for about a minute.
- Open the eyes and conclude the meditation.
- With practice, you can increase the breath count from seven to ten or even twenty.

The above is only one example of many chakra meditations available to us. We can easily make up our own. Each chakra has a symbolic colour (two, in fact if we count the traditional Hindu colours, rather than the "New-age" colours I have used above), symbol and bija mantra. They are all listed in the chart below (figure 17). Which we use or don't use is entirely a matter of personal choice, though the detail of the symbols are hard to memorise, so perhaps better left to experienced meditators or those with a good visual memory. I have also taken the liberty of including the traditionally associated elements in the chart. We do not use these in chakra balancing and therapy but I am aware that some readers may wish to integrate chakra therapy into some other therapy and that identifying the elements could therefore be useful.

A more advanced (and highly effective) version of the previous meditation is given below. It gets round the problem of remembering details of the symbols. We only have to remember the number of petals, which are given in boxes next to the symbols in figure. 18.

- Assume a comfortable seated position. Make sure the hands are comfortable and not fidgety.
- Close the eyes. Observe the breathing passively, without trying to change it.
- Focus the attention onto the first chakra. Visualise it as a red, four petal flower of exquisite beauty.
- Breathing naturally and continuing to visualise, count seven out breaths.
- Now shift the attention up to the second chakra. Visualise it as an orange, six petal flower.
- Count seven out breaths.
- Work up the chakras using the colours red, orange, yellow, green blue and purple and finally, white for chakra seven (crown).
- The petal numbers are 4, 6,10,12,16, 2 and infinity respectively.
- Do the same working down from the crown to the root, using a lower number of out-breaths if you wish.
- Stop counting and just observe the breath for about a minute.
- Open the eyes and conclude the meditation.
- With practice, you can increase the breath count from seven to ten or even twenty.
- If desired, the traditional colours shown on the chart can be used instead of the new age colours.

Figure 17 Chakras – colours, elements and bija mantras.

CHAKRA	BIJA	TRADITIONAL COLOUR	"NEW AGE" COLOUR	ELEMENT
7.	Aum	White light	White	—
6.	Aum	Silver	Purple	—
5.	Ham	Violet	Blue	Space ether
4.	Yam	Blue	Green	Air
3.	Ram	Yellow	Yellow	Fire
2.	Vam	Crimson	Orange	Water
1.	Lam	Deep red	Red	Earth

Regular meditation helps to awaken our creative and problem solving potential, as well as being a great stress management tool, life aid and mental hygiene practice. Anyone can benefit from it. You do not have to take on board any religion or philosophy you are uncomfortable with. An atheist can gain just as much benefit as a devout Buddhist. Incidentally, there is an ancient and unbroken tradition of Christian, Judaic and Islamic meditation – it is not just the cultural property of Indian and Chinese belief systems. *Basic meditation skills need to be mastered before attempting chakra meditations.* Meditation is no different from any other activity in this respect – it gets better with practice. It is best in the early stages not to be too ambitious from a time standpoint. Three minutes well focussed is much better than half an hour with the mind wandering here and there, like a badly trained dog let off the lead. I started with five minute sessions and very slowly increased the time span to fifteen minutes over a period of several months, though I do occasionally have longer sessions.

Figure 18 Chakras – traditional symbols.

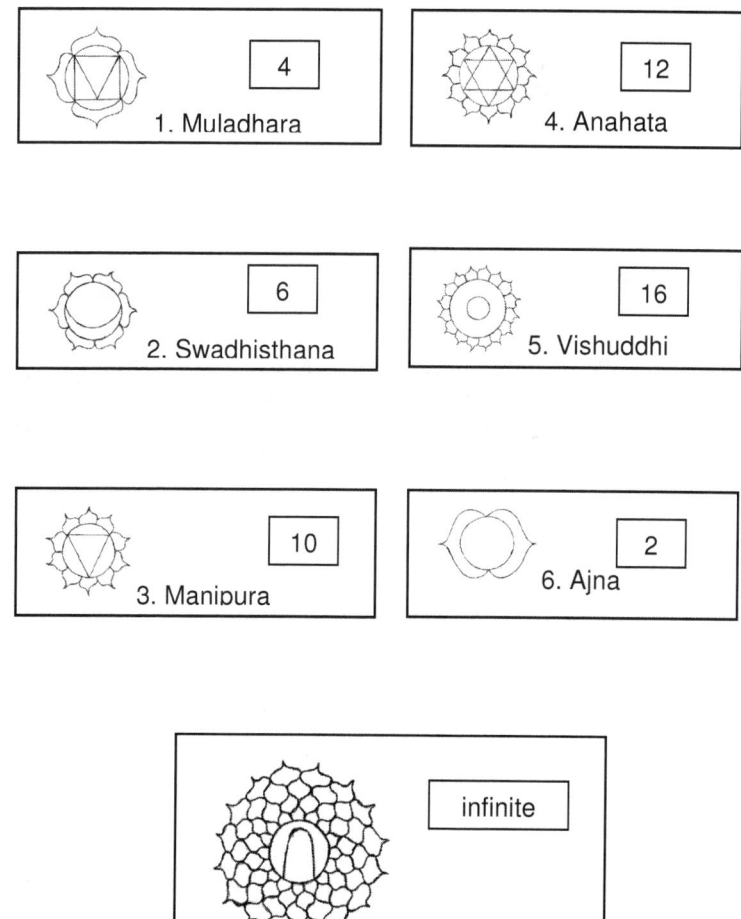

A gentle word of warning about meditation courses - some have a religious agenda, sometimes overt but often concealed. If that agenda coincides with your own, it's unlikely to be a problem. If it doesn't, you may find yourself in a state of emotional conflict that is difficult to resolve. Ask a few questions first and don't spend more money than you can afford to write off, if things don't work out for you. Many courses are, of course completely non-sectarian and secular and it would be most unfair to tar them all with the "dodgy guru" brush. Also, those who do have an overt agenda (often Buddhist) don't necessarily put any pressure on participants to convert. Some courses are free of charge or operate on a donation basis. *Caveat Emptor!*[1]

Another gentle warning – it is most unwise to focus on one chakra only in meditation, unless there is a compelling reason to do so, for example, if it is severely depleted. To do so tends to cause a pranic overcharge in that part of the body. A common mistake, due to its association with unconditional love, is to focus only on the heart chakra. This can cause a localised overcharge, causing the heart to work too hard and eventually to cardiovascular disease. Always focus on all the chakras (though one at a time) but emphasising one by spending more time on it if necessary.

---

[1] "Let the buyer beware" – an old legal maxim.

18. CRYSTALS

The world of crystals is a fascinating and beautiful one. There is a mysterious inner logic to their structure, which many (including myself) find irresistible. If I had the space at home and the money, I'd buy a large display cabinet and start collecting. However, we must also ask the question, are they of any use, therapeutically speaking? I have to confess to a degree of scepticism. There are many things in this world that are beautiful and command our respect but that does not mean that they have therapeutic value. The music I am listening to as I write this inspires and uplifts me but it does not stop the nagging and persistent cough that I am presently suffering from. However, if I place one finger on my throat chakra and another on my heart chakra and hold them in that position for about a minute, the cough eases. *Results count for more than theory and belief* is the clear message of that story, though some might argue that my little "creative first aid" technique works because I believe in it! Further, there is almost as much nonsense written about crystals as there is about chakras. I once had a revealing conversation with a crystal and gemstone retailer, whose considerable knowledge and helpfulness commanded my respect. He had been collecting and dealing in crystals for many years. He showed me a popular paperback on the subject, which contained several glaring factual errors he had found, simply in a casual and brief perusal. He had some withering comments to make about both book and author.

However, there is (as always), another side to the story. It only occurred to me quite recently and I have to cheerfully confess that I do not speak from a position of scientific expertise. I had to test the memory banks severely and go right back to school chemistry lessons over half a century ago. Some crystals have water locked into their molecular structure but this is usually ignored as it is not really relevant from a chemical standpoint. For example, blue copper sulphate (not used in crystal therapy) has the chemical formula $CuSO_4.5H_2O$. If it is heated, it turns white because "$5H_2O$" has evaporated, so it is usually simply given the formula CuSO4 by chemists and science teachers. It is likely that some crystals used by therapists have similar water molecules locked into their structure and many more minerals (most, in fact) have silicon in their molecular structure. Silicon is the earth's most common element. Neither of these substances radiates much detectable prana, using the life energy meter. Using various borrowed crystals and minerals, I was unable to get more than a 10% deflection. A piece of wood that had been lying in my shed for over two years produced a 35% deflection. However, both water and silicon have the property of *absorbing* prana in the manner of an "energy sponge". The reasoning behind this assertion is too lengthy and complex to go into in this volume, which is more about therapy than "alternative" science. Now, if we are sick, it is likely that we have pools of stagnant, blocked energy in our body. Wilhelm Reich (see chapter 2) called this phenomenon DOR *(Deadly ORgone)*. My theory now (which I admit is partly speculative) is that crystals and minerals *may* have therapeutic value but not in the way that most healers believe. They do not *radiate* a positive, life giving energy but *absorb* a toxic energy. For this reason, they should always be washed under a running tap before and after use. So, if crystals are "your thing", go ahead, but remember that a lot of the information "out there" is suspect and the result of guesswork and cut and paste thinking. Some "experts" are only expert at appearing to be expert! Keep up your own research and keep detailed notes of what works and what doesn't is the best option. Also, we cannot escape a fact that some find uncomfortable (though I personally am quite relaxed about it and intrigued by it), namely that if we and/or our clients *think* that something works, it probably will!

Therapists who use crystals usually place them on some or all of the chakras and occasionally on other parts of the body, especially parts that are injured or diseased. They are left there for a few minutes, sometimes longer, while the client relaxes. They are sometimes used in conjunction with sound or coloured light. For the record, those listed below are sometimes recommended as being effective, though that claim is not my own. The colours are significant. They correspond roughly with the "new age", symbolic colours listed in chapter 16. At the risk of seeming doctrinaire, I must remind readers about common errors concerning the location of the major chakras and the variability of their positions. Good mapping is once again essential if we are using crystals in conjunction with chakras.

CHAKRA	CRYSTAL
1. ROOT	Black tourmaline, smoky quartz, bloodstone, hematite, onyx, pipestone.
2. SACRAL	Carnelian/sard, red jasper, cuprite.
3. NAVEL	Citrine, sulphur, gold, yellow calcite.
4. HEART	Aventurine, green tourmaline, green apophyllite, malachite, rose quartz.
5. THROAT	Blue lace agate, blue topaz, celestite.
6. BROW	Amethyst, lapis lazuli, sugulite, azurite.
7. CROWN	Clear quartz, rutilated quartz, any clear crystal.

I am aware that a lot of this brief chapter is rather speculative but underneath the speculation is a modest seasoning of hard facts. However, we still have a lot to learn (or maybe unlearn) about the power and effects of crystals and minerals. If you disagree with me, that's OK – feel free to ignore or adapt this chapter!

19. SEX AND SEXUALITY

What has sex got to do with chakra therapy? Rather a lot, I would argue. Even in these (allegedly) enlightened times, sex is the "elephant in the living room" from a therapeutic and well-being standpoint. Yet we still pussyfoot around the issue "like Queen Victoria stepping round a dogturd"[1], unless the client actually presents with a sexual problem. It would be unfair to say that the presenting symptom is fake or imaginary – it almost certainly won't be but quite often the symptoms distract from or mask an underlying *bioenergetic* (i.e. emotional) problem.   For instance, a recurring sore throat can (though not necessarily does) suggest a chronic sense of sadness and urge to cry. Consider carefully the following points, mostly already covered but rather disparately –

- Prana (life energy) is the fuel of the chakras.
- Prana is a tangible force. *It is also emotional and sexual energy.* A person with depleted life energy is also likely to be sexually debilitated and emotionally reserved.
- As pranic levels decline in old age, interest in sex declines.
- The male erection and its female equivalent, dilation and moistening of the vagina, is not just the result of increased blood flow, though that is part of the story. It is also caused by an accumulation of prana in the pelvic and genital region. This accumulation can be thought of as the libido. If this arousal is not at least partially discharged by sexual activity, a sexual stasis eventually causes (or rather, reinforces) neurosis and other psychosomatic problems.[2]
- In energetic terms, orgasm is not just a discharge of sexual fluids; it is a discharge of prana. It is not just about reproduction.

---

[1] This memorable metaphor was created by my brother Peter Jones, concerning the closely related subject of orgone (life-energy).
[2] Reich, W. *The Function of the Orgasm.*

- It is perfectly possible to survive within a celibate lifestyle but our emotional and creative lives are severely diminished and impoverished. *Prana is also creative energy.* Beethoven, Shakespeare and Picasso could not have achieved what they did without a high pranic charge. Celibate people are rarely creative.
- Sex and spirituality are *not* incompatible. Indeed, they are mutually enriching.
- Sex repression and denial is a favourite tool of all oppressive political and social institutions and has been for millennia. It is the control system par excellence. If a spiritual teacher urges celibacy, he's probably up to no good!

The above is a précis of what is actually a complex story but suffices for our purposes. It follows that we simply cannot ignore sex within a therapeutic context – or within our own context of well-being. We must ask of ourselves and our client a simple question, namely "are our needs being met?" This presents us with practical and ethical problems. The obvious first is – how do we broach the subject with a client without seeming nosey, prurient or intrusive? What if the client has experienced years of abstinence and the whole thing is a touchy and embarrassing subject they would rather avoid? What if their cultural background is profoundly sex-negative and guilt prone – or even abusive?

It may well be that we will be unable to help the client, as their problems and attitudes are too deeply ingrained. All we can then do is to alleviate a little, rather than cure. If the client fails to mention the subject, we should not raise it early in the treatment, even if the client is only planning on two or three appointments. They are obviously not ready to discuss it. If they keep coming back, it is likely that you will repeatedly observe that one or both of the lower two chakras are "down" or unbalanced and stimulation and balancing only works temporarily. This is our cue to make polite enquiries about their relationship (or lack of one). We can point out that the two lowest chakras (especially the sacral chakra) are related to what we now call libido. If the client's relationship is poor or non-existent, it might be better to refer them to an experienced sexual/marital counsellor, unless you have such training yourself, of course. A course in counselling skills, if you have not already had such training, is a very useful supplement to almost any complementary therapy training.

Meanwhile, we all need to bear in mind four important points. Firstly, almost any legal, non-exploitative sexual activity, not associated with guilt, is better than none. Secondly, a relationship does not have to be "live in" – plenty of couples enjoy loving, sexual relationships, which are "semi-detached", though it must be admitted that this is not ideal. Thirdly, it is usually better to end a bad relationship, rather than endure it, though that is a decision that must be made by the client, without undue prodding by the therapist. "Remember – you have a choice" is a good, non-pushy way of expressing this. Many individuals of both sexes find that walking away from a long-standing but unhappy relationship gives them a huge confidence and morale boost, enabling them to find another, healthier relationship more easily than they thought possible. Fourthly, we are all imperfect specimens of humanity. Mr or Ms Perfect does not exist. Many of us have absurdly high expectations when it comes to selecting a mate. Everyone they meet is not beautiful, rich, well-dressed, charming, clever, witty or sexy enough. Today, we are in the sad and paradoxical situation of having record amounts of relationship dissatisfaction with record numbers of people with no relationship at all, or only a very tenuous one. "Get real" are two words of useful advice for the latter section of the populace. All this applies whether we are male or female, straight, gay or bi.

A final important point. If the client is very touchy and defensive about sex or maybe talks about it obsessively or self righteously, he/she may possibly have suffered sexual abuse – though this is (in my view) rare and it is easy to become simplistic in this diagnosis. Their attitude may have other, more mundane reasons behind it. What we must *never* do is to implant a vulnerable and suggestible client with the idea of abuse, which they have not actually suffered. An unwary therapist can easily do this if they use any type of hypnotic/suggestive technique. We must also remember that troubled people sometimes make untrue (or highly exaggerated) allegations. A blanket, knee-jerk acceptance of a dramatic claim is just as unhelpful as a knee-jerk denial and disbelief. This is most definitely a minefield best explored by a trained specialist. In recent years, Western countries have got caught up in a moral panic about child abuse, which is understandable but unhelpful. We cannot, however abandon the client. We can continue with the chakra balancing described in this book, while urging them to seek specialist treatment. If, as a therapist, you are troubled by vague suspicions, a casual "is there anything else you want to tell me about all this?" might elicit further information. If no further information is forthcoming, a diplomatic silence is probably wiser, unless we have the training to deal with the distressing material which may emerge.

20. ASSORTED HINTS AND TIPS.

I was tempted to call this chapter "dos and don'ts" but as a devout anti-authoritarian, decided that was unwise! Seriously, though – it is very easy (and counter-productive) to slide into a narrow, doctrinaire, "I know best" approach when, at least in chakra therapy, the very opposite is required, namely, a creative and independent spirit. So this chapter is offered in the sincere hope that it will prove helpful, rather than as a rule-book. There are only two basic "no compromise" rules – treat your client the way you would like to be treated, ethically and with compassion and remember the old medical maxim (often ignored), "at least, do no harm" - and do the same to yourself, please.

- Keep yourself in good shape, both physically and mentally, with a lively energy system. Much of your success depends on good energy interaction between client and therapist.

- Make sure you remind the client to keep breathing deeply but without forcing. Do the same yourself.

- Make sure you are both in a comfortable working position.

- Ask your client if they have had a proper clinical investigation by a doctor or (if appropriate) a trained physiotherapist, osteopath or chiropractor. If they haven't (which is unlikely), urge them to do so but don't refuse to treat them in the meantime.

- Further to the above, you can offer an "energy diagnosis" but not a medical one. That is a task for a doctor.

- *Never* advise a client to discontinue a medical or other complementary treatment. That is their decision to make.

Explain what you are doing and why, without too much tedious detail. Explain why you may be working on part of the body that is well away from the apparent problem area and why you may appear to be doing very little, except touching.

- Keep a spare pendulum. They occasionally get lost or the chain gets tangled into a knot.

- Hold the pendulum under a cold, running tap for a few seconds before and after a treatment to disperse any negative energy. Do the same with crystals, if you use them.

- Be prepared to experiment a bit.

- A little humility is called for, without overdoing it. Don't make exaggerated claims and remember that you can't know everything. If a client presents with an illness you have never heard of, say "you can teach me something here, what is xyz?" or words to that effect. Remind them that your job is not to cure the specifics but to boost and balance the client's own natural healing energies.

- Keep good but concise records.

21. SUMMARY AND CONCLUSIONS

- Chakras are life energy centres or vortices situated in the core of the body but manifesting externally. They are sometimes called psycho-physical centres.

- We have seen that the chakras manifest in a fluid way, depending on the observer and the health and emotional state of the client. A flexible and creative approach is therefore required of the therapist.

- The fuel for the chakra system is prana (known by many other names), drawn into the body mainly through the breath and circulated round the body through energy channels called nadis.

- Where the principal nadis cross, there is a "hotspot" or chakra, which radiates prana outwards to the periphery.

- There are seven major chakras and many more minor chakras.

- The major chakras and most of the minor chakras can be located and tested by means of a dowsing pendulum.

- The major chakras can be stimulated by both "hands off" and "hands on" movements and balanced with gentle finger pressure on the chakras and their associated minor chakras.

- There are a number of other techniques available to us, including meditation, traditional yoga postures, breathwork and other exercises.

- The principal objective of chakra therapy and balancing is to raise prana levels and improve flow, both locally and in the entire organism to accelerate and facilitate natural healing and recovery.

- Chakra therapy can be used independently or in conjunction with other therapies.

It follows from the above that chakra therapy is neither complex nor arcane – despite the efforts of some to make it so. It can be easily learnt and practiced as a "stand alone" therapy, or in conjunction with other therapies. Much of it can be practiced on a "DIY" basis, though the services of a trained therapist are preferable. No drugs, natural or otherwise are used and minimal equipment is required. There is no therapy known to this author that is in any way incompatible with chakra therapy. It would be dishonest to tout the therapy as some kind of "miracle cure" (in my view, there is no such thing) but the healing potential for almost any illness is considerable. Further, we do not have to have any clinical symptoms at all to benefit. Many people feel vaguely ill at ease, anxious or generally "low" and lacking vitality. Sooner or later, an illness will manifest itself but chakra therapy and balancing can help to nip this in the bud. Prevention is always better than cure and the potential in this area is considerable.

The author runs courses and day seminars on chakra therapy and a number of other related subjects. He can be contacted via his website –

<u>www.yogacollege.co.uk</u>

BIBLIOGRAPHY

Cross, John R. *Healing with the Chakra Energy System.*
ISBN 978-1-55643-625-3

DeMeo, J. *The Orgone Accumulator Handbook.*
ISBN 0-9621855-0-7

Gimbutas, M. *The Language of the Goddess.*
ISBN 0-500-28249-8

Jones, J. *A Yoga Garland.* ISBN 0-9551076-2-8

Jones, P. *A Seed Germination Experiment with the Orgone Accumulator.* CORE. www.orgonomyuk.org.uk

Jones, P. *How toBuild andUse Your Own Orgone energy Accumulator.* www.orgonomyuk.org.uk

LeShan, L. *How to Meditate.* ISBN 0-553-24453-1

Saradananda, Swami. *Chakra Meditation.*
ISBN 978-1-84483-445-7

Lowen, A. *The Way to Vibrant Health.*
ISBN 978-0-9743737-1-3

Motoyama, Hiroshi. *Theories of the Chakras.*
ISBN 978-81-7822-023-9

Muktibodhananda, Swami. *Swara Yoga – the Tantric Science of Brain Breathing.* ISBN 978-81-85787-36-7

Reich, W. *The Cancer Biopathy.* ISBN 0-374-51014-8

Reich, W. *The Bioelectrical Investigation of Sexuality and Anxiety.* ISBN 0-374-51728-2

Reich, W. *The Bion Experiments.* ISBN 0-374-51446-1

Reich, W. *Character Analysis.* ISBN 0-374-50980-8

Reich, W. *The Function of the Orgasm.* Noonday Press.

Satyananda Saraswati, Swami. *Asana Pranayama Mudra Bandha.* ISBN 81-86336-14-1

Satyananda Saraswati, Swami. *Kundalini Tantra.* ISBN 81-85787-15-8

Sharaf, M. *Fury on Earth.* ISBN 0-312-31370-5

Zhang Yu Huan and Ken Rose. *A Brief History of Qi.* ISBN 0-912111-63-1

OTHER RESOURCES

www.yogacollege.co.uk This is the author's website. Any e-mail comments, favourable or otherwise, are welcome. Information on courses, classes, workshops etc., mainly (but not exclusively) in or near Essex, UK. If you're based abroad, I am not far from London Stansted airport.

www.namaskaram.co.uk The on-line magazine of the Independent Yoga Network. Lots of interesting yoga-related articles, news and "what's on".

www.heliognosis.com Makers of the life energy meter and other research equipment. Canada based but they ship to most countries.

www.thecrystalman.co.uk Crystal retailers and suppliers of inexpensive dowsing pendula. Based in Glastonbury, UK.

www.orgonomyuk.org.uk CORE is the Centre for Orgonomic Research and Education. Lots of info on courses, research, inexpensive publications, on-line help etc. about the science of life energy. Based in Preston, UK.

www.orgonelab.org The Orgone Biophysical Research Laboratory site. Nothing on chakras but lots of interesting and controversial stuff on orgone/life energy.

www.naturalenergywork.net Retail offshoot of the above. Research equipment, books and lots more. Oregon, USA based but will ship world-wide.

GLOSSARY OF TERMS USED

"**S**" denotes Sanskrit, a classical Indian Language. "**C**" denotes Chinese, "**J**" denotes Japanese. "**M**" denotes modern English medical terminology. Sanskrit and Chinese spellings tend to vary.

Acupoint. A small energy "hotspot" situated on a meridian and used by acupuncturists and other meridian therapists. An established part of traditional Chinese medicine (TCM) for millennia.

Alimentary tract (M). The entire length of "plumbing" between mouth and anus, through which all food must pass on its digestive journey.

Anterior (M). Towards the front of the body.

Āyurveda (S). Traditional Indian medicine.

Āsana (S). A yoga posture.

ANS (M). See autonomic nervous system.

Autonomic nervous system (M). The body's instinctive, "primitive" nervous system, which helps to regulate the internal organs automatically, without conscious control.

Bija mantra (S). (bija="seed"). A single syllable mantra reputed to open and stimulate a specific chakra.

Bilateral (M). Towards both sides of the body.

Bindu (S). A point or dot. In this text, it refers to a point on the skull just back from the crown, identified by a very small indentation.

Cardiovascular System (M). The heart, arteries, veins and other blood vessels.

Chakra (S). An energy vortex or "hotspot" in the central core of the body, radiating outwards.

Double blind. An experimental technique, where neither the subject nor the observer know whether the medication or procedure is active or placebo, so neither can be unconsciously influenced.

Dowsing pendulum. A pendulum with a short chain (usually about 20 cm) and a crystal or shaped piece of mineral attached to one end.

Chi (C). See qi.

Chikung (C). See qigong.

GP. General practitioner. The "frontline" doctor in the UK.

Hatha Yoga (S). The physical yoga of postures, breathwork etc. Hatha Yoga comes in many styles from the very gentle to the highly athletic.

Ida/pingala (S). Two of the three principal nadis, which are believed to wind round the third (sushumna) in a double helix.

Jala Neti (S). Nasal irrigation.

Kriya (S). Deed or act. It usually refers to yogic cleansing practices.

Kundalini (S). "She who is coiled" – the mythical, sleeping, female serpent coiled three and a half times round the muladhara (root) chakra. When awakened, she rushes up the spine, piercing the chakras and triggering enlightenment. She can also be thought of as the "Goddess within".

Lateral (M). Towards the side of the body.

Lesion (M). Damage or injury. Unhealthy change in the function or texture of part of an organ, bone etc.

Mantra (S). A chant or sacred sound, usually repeated many times.

Medial (M). Towards the middle of the body.

Meridian. An energy pathway in the body, usually near the periphery. English terminology but usually used in Traditional Chinese Medicine and related disciplines.

Musculoskeletal System (M). The bones, muscles and connective tissues e.g. tendons.

Nādī (S). An energy channel or pathway, usually in the central core of the body.

Orac. An abbreviation of –

Orgone Energy Accumulator. A six sided cabinet or box, made from alternating layers of organic material and ferrous metal. It accumulates the atmospheric orgone (see below), so it can be used therapeutically and for research.

Orgone. Life energy as rediscovered, harnessed and defined by Wilhelm Reich. Also the primordial animating force of the universe.

Orgonomy. The scientific study and investigation of the orgone.

Orthosypathetic (M). The "fight or flight" part of the ANS. Also called sympathetic.

Parasympathetic (M). The opposing part of the ANS, dealing with rest, regeneration and relaxation responses.

Perineum (M). A piece of connective tissue in the pelvic floor, in front of the anus and behind the vagina or scrotum.

Placebo (M). "I will please". Usually refers to an inert medication or procedure, whose results are then compared with those of an active medication or procedure to test its efficacy. Also occasionally used to keep a difficult patient happy!

Posterior (M). Towards the back of the body.

Prāna (S). Life energy, life force, breath.

Prānāyāma (S). Extension of the breath/life force. Yogic breathing techniques.

Prone. Lying flat on the stomach.

Qi (C). Life energy. See prana.

Qigong (C). "Energy cultivation". A Chinese "breath and movement" exercise system.

Shakti (S) The wife or consort of Shiva. The female principle.

Shiva (S). The Hindu god of destruction and regeneration. The cosmic dancer. The male principle.

Supine. Lying flat on the back.

Sushumna (S). The principal, central nadi.

Swara (S). "Sound". The dynamic balance between ida and pingala nadis and their associated nostrils. The sound in the nostrils associated with that balance.

TCM. An abbreviation of "Traditional Chinese Medicine".

Tsubo (J). An acupoint as described in Japanese healing methods, such as shiatsu.

Unilateral (M). Towards one side of the body.

Vertebra (M). A hollow bone in the spinal column, through which the spinal cord passes. *(Plural vertebrae).*

Yogi or yogin (S). Anyone who practices yoga. A female yogi is a yogini.

INDEX